Advance Praise f

"*Embody* is a powerful addition to the Health at Every Size® community. It brings to life what we know from scientific evidence: people of all sizes can live active and healthy lives—and love themselves, too!"

—Linda Bacon, PhD, Author of *Health At Every Size*

"*Embody* belongs in every school, home, and place where the lives of our boys and girls matter!"

—Carol Bloom, LCSW, Co-Founder of the Women's Therapy Centre Institute, New York

"With *Embody*, people of all ages can learn that self-love is the best motivation there is to care for their uniquely beautiful bodies. I am excited to share this wonderful resource with my clients."

—Carmen Cool, MA, LPC, Psychotherapist, Boulder, CO

"*Embody* sparks a flame of self-love in your heart that glows brighter when you share it with others. It makes you want to stand up and say, 'I am beauty!'"

—Jessica Diaz, MSW, Founder of Love Guerrillas

"A beautiful, wise, practical book that will empower a next generation to shed our culture of toxic ideas of perfectionism and bodily dissatisfaction. This book, and The Body Positive movement, are part of a compassionate revolution leading people to greater dignity and empowerment."

—Dacher Keltner, PhD, Founding Director, Greater Good Science Center, UC Berkeley

embody

embody

LEARNING TO LOVE
YOUR UNIQUE BODY
(and quiet that
critical voice!)

CONNIE SOBCZAK

FOREWORD BY ELIZABETH SCOTT, LCSW

gürze books

EMBODY
Learning to Love your Unique Body
(and quiet that critical voice!)

© 2014 by Connie Sobczak

Gürze Books
P.O. Box 2238
Carlsbad, CA 92018
760-434-7533
www.gurzebooks.com

Cover and interior design by Anita Koury
anitakourydesign.com

Library of Congress Cataloging-in-Publication Data

Sobczak, Connie.
Embody : learning to love your unique body (and quiet that critical voice!)
/ Connie Sobczak ; foreword by Elizabeth Scott.
pages cm
ISBN 978-0-936077-80-2 (paperback)
ISBN 978-0-936077-81-9 (ebook)
1. Body image. 2. Eating disorders. 3. Self-esteem. I. Title.
BF697.5.B63S63 2014
306.4'613--dc23

2014007894

NOTE:
The author and publisher of this book intend for this publication
to provide accurate information.
It is sold with the understanding that it is meant to complement,
not substitute for, professional medical and/or
psychological services.

Printed in the USA on 100% PCW recycled paper.

1 3 4 5 9 0 8 6 4 2

Embody is dedicated to
Jim, Carmen, Mom, and Elizabeth
for their endless love, support, and inspiration.
Neither The Body Positive nor this book
would exist without them!

In memory of Bill Earle, my sweet papa
who gave me his love of writing,
a keen interest in people's stories,
and the awesome ability to pay attention
to the smallest of details.

Contents

Foreword

One stormy November day, Connie Sobczak and I led a Body Positive leadership training with fifty high school students, counselors, and teachers. One by one, the participants stood up to speak out loud about what makes them beautiful. Through tears they talked about the pain of feeling ugly, invisible, of being insulted by the confusing and hurtful messages they had received throughout their lives. But, bravely, each person took a risk to challenge these messages and to choose, instead, to inhabit and declare their own beauty. A girl spoke about the beauty she inherited from her Mexican grandmother that was expressed in her resilience and her wide, strong back. Before reading a poem he had written, a teacher shared his realization that, as a man, he had never been asked to think about his beauty and how difficult it was to use the word to describe himself. A counselor passed around photos of her two beloved children as she talked about the love and gratitude she feels for her belly, with its fat and stretch marks imprinted by the miracle of the beings who had emerged from within.

Deep pain and great power exist side by side in our associations with our bodies and our beauty. Do you think about your relationship with your physical form? Are you aware that it is a connection that can be positively transformed? The book you hold in your hands offers you the opportunity to move first into the struggles you may experience in relationship to your beauty, health, and identity, and then, out the other side to the joy and confidence that come from accepting what you cannot change and celebrating who you truly are.

Your body is the seat of your intuition; it is the avenue through which you connect to your gut instincts—to what you *know*. Intuition is the most reliable authority to guide the choices you make. Your body talks to you in sensations; feelings of tension, fear, hunger, pleasure, aliveness, and pain are just some of the ways it attempts to communicate with you. This is why staying connected to your physical self—*with as little conflict as possible*—is fundamental to health and wellbeing.

If you spend copious amounts of energy attempting to diminish your body, or if your imagination is limited such that you cannot see beauty in yourself, then you become disconnected from the world around you. You lose perspective and purpose. Building a loving relationship with your body lets you disengage from these struggles and expand your vision. You can then uncover a genuine confidence and pursue the unique role you play in transforming the world into something that is whole and beautiful.

Embody: Learning to Love Your Unique Body (and quiet that critical voice!) is an invitation to you to join the vibrant community of The Body Positive. In reading this book and working with the practices, you have an opportunity to connect to wonderful, natural resources available within you, such as self-love, intuition, strength, and receptiveness. You can become free of any shame you feel about your appearance, shame that isolates and paralyzes so many people with eating and body image problems. With this freedom you transform your relationship with your body to one of trust and compassion. You may further decide you want to speak openly about your suffering, thus breaking the isolation of others who are locked in the downward spiral of body hatred. In doing so, you become part of a movement for positive change in the world.

. . .

For seventeen years I have worked alongside the author of this book, Connie Sobczak. Together we have helped thousands of individuals heal their relationships with their bodies, food, and exercise, and built Body Positive communities nationwide through workshops, leadership trainings, and distribution of our creative educational materials.

Connie brings a patient, compassionate, and loving soul to this work. She carries the wisdom that comes from suffering loss and choosing to seek out purpose and love—instead of despair. Connie's intimate and powerful story is woven throughout to inspire you to reach for the same fierce commitment to kindness for your body that she models. The intense caring she feels for others is genuine; her spontaneous humor and vibrant aliveness fill the world with joy and laughter. You can depend on Connie. Take your time while you read her words. Explore the practices to uncover your own insights. Utilize the information in this book that speaks to you and overlook the rest. Listen to your body—it knows what is best for you.

Warmly,
Elizabeth

Elizabeth Scott, LCSW,
Co-Founder, The Body Positive

em·body (*verb*): provide a spirit with a physical form

Introduction

"Doubt yourself and you doubt everything you see. Judge your-self and you see judges everywhere. But if you listen to the sound of your own voice, you can rise above doubt and judgment. And you can see forever."

—Nancy Lopez

Imagine living in a world where people possess genuine self-love and are free to experience their own authentic beauty—a world where a compassionate, forgiving voice is consistently brought forth to counteract self-criticism, where having an appetite for life is both honored and valued. This is the world of The Body Positive. It is more than the name of a nonprofit organization; it is a state of mind and a growing cultural movement that offers people the opportunity to put down the burdens of judgment, comparison, and shame in order to cultivate a relationship with themselves that is built on a foundation of self-love and trust.

When we become "embodied"—choosing to live consciously in our bodies and thereby giving our spirits a physical home— we can experience love for our "flawed" human selves. This love gives us access to our brilliant intuitive wisdom, which can guide the decisions we make each day. It is through self-love and deep listening that we are able to unleash the natural creative energy we all possess—a life force that can be used to make the world a better place to live in the biggest and smallest of ways. The individuals who inhabit the expanding Body Positive community use their time, energy, and brainpower to make positive changes in their own lives and to support the healing of others, vital resources once devoted to perfecting their physical image and feeding self-hatred.

THE PASSION BEHIND THE PURPOSE

A primary motivator for creating The Body Positive was my desire to help people avoid the same painful road I took that led to a six-year eating disorder. The seeds of my suffering were planted at the age of thirteen when my sister Stephanie and most of my friends began dieting because they thought something was wrong with their bodies. Being younger than Stephanie and all of my peers, and possessing a strong desire to fit in, I was easily influenced by the actions of others. Two years later, I followed through on a suggestion from a friend to purge the food I had just eaten. Though there was no name for it in the mid-1970s, many people I knew were engaging in bulimia.

By the time I was nineteen, the eating disorder had taken over my life. The struggles I experienced prompted my leave from the University of California at Berkeley and destroyed my longstanding dream of becoming a computer engineer. Over the next two years I returned to the university twice, each time with a new major. My eating disorder fooled me into believing my course of study was the problem during both of these attempts to resume my education. Again and again, I dropped out of school until I finally realized something was wrong with *me*, not my intellectual pursuits, and took time off to heal. By the age of twenty-two, bulimia was part of my past. I eventually enrolled in another college and graduated with a bachelor's degree in psychology.

I am grateful that true and complete recovery from my eating disorder was possible. I learned to nurture an inner strength that helped me realize my existence was precious and worth fighting for, but my life was changed forever. The suffering I experienced over my body radically shifted the course of my career and life purpose.

That purpose became clear a decade later when Stephanie died at age thirty-six from the physical consequences of her obsession with thinness and "ideal" beauty. Stephanie's downward spiral began in her late teens when she escalated her dieting behaviors by joining Weight Watchers. She underwent the typical weight loss/weight regain cycle experienced by most dieters, and, not surprisingly, developed bulimia. Though Stephanie and I did not begin our eating disorders together, we soon discovered we were both practicing the same behaviors. We supported one another in our desire to lose weight, often engaging in the binge/purge ritual together.

Ironically, it was Stephanie who helped me heal. In 1982, she won a free trip for two to Hawaii and took me with her. I was standing at the edge of recovery, so I told her I would not go on the trip if she planned to practice bulimia. Each night we ate different foods in moderation, especially those that had prompted binges for us in the past. Every morning we stood in front of the hotel mirror in our bathing suits and offered a true reflection to one another. Though we couldn't see ourselves objectively, we could see each other. The words of support and love my sister gave me on that trip were exactly what I needed to complete my healing. Unfortunately, Stephanie came home and resumed her bulimia immediately.

Stephanie's physical size wasn't her only preoccupation with her body. She believed that her nipples were deformed and made the decision to get them surgically "fixed." The plastic surgeon suggested, and Stephanie agreed, that she also get implants since her breasts were going to be cut open anyway. The operation was done in the late 1970s, a time when the general public was unaware of the potentially harmful side effects of silicone implants. Unfortunately, the left implant hardened. The surgeon's solution was to soften it by using his and another doctor's hands to crush Stephanie's breast.

Unknown to anyone for more than ten years, silicone had oozed out of the implant and poisoned Stephanie's body. She developed *Lupus Erythematosis*, an autoimmune disease that caused her to experience extreme joint pain. Numerous doctors attempted to ease her suffering without success because they did not identify the Lupus. She was on heavy pain medication throughout most of her twenties and into her thirties. All the while, Stephanie still had her eating disorder, which caused her to be perpetually under-nourished. When a rheumatologist finally diagnosed the Lupus, Stephanie's organs were already severely compromised. The steroids she took to combat her disease further damaged her health. The "official" cause of her death was "electrolyte imbalance due to renal failure due to Systemic Lupus Erythematosis," with malnutrition listed as an additional contributor. When people ask me what happened to my sister, I tell them she died because she was at war with her body. To me, this explanation is closest to the truth.

My daughter, Carmen, was a year old when Stephanie died, an age at which she was wildly in love with her body. She was thrilled with her mastery of walking; she delighted in naming her body parts, especially her round belly and belly button. Eating food was a nurturing and playful experience for Carmen. Her intuitive self knew exactly what her physical needs were, and she demanded to have those needs met. Carmen was—as most toddlers are—free to take pleasure in all aspects of her body.

Stephanie's death prompted me to question if it was possible to raise a child free from body hatred in a society so focused on image and physical perfection. Though long healed from my own problems with my body and self-image, I still worried that I would somehow cause Carmen to develop an eating disorder, or that societal messages would lure her into the traps that had caught me as a girl. It was then that I made the commitment to change the world for my daughter. Grandiose as that may sound, my fierce maternal instincts led me on an exploration of what that declaration truly meant.

It took several years before my direction became clear: I envisioned using my creative skills and personal experience to produce videos about body image for teen audiences. This was at a time when conversations with teenagers regarding how they felt about their bodies were much less common than they are today. My goal was to provide them with the messages—delivered by their peers—that both self-love and a peaceful relationship with food and exercise were entirely possible. Shortly thereafter, I formed The Body Positive as a nonprofit organization and met Elizabeth Scott. The organization has become so much more than I ever envisioned, and a great deal of that has to do with our partnership.

Elizabeth is passionate about her work because she believes that a healthy self-image is an essential aspect of a person's development. She credits her mother Lynn, a feminist therapist, for communicating a positive message about women's bodies that allowed her to grow up with an abundance of self-love. Elizabeth's discovery of African dance as a teenager and her exploration of improvisational dance throughout her life sustain a great appreciation for her body and its capacity to express pleasure and vitality.

As a therapist, Elizabeth's commitment to The Body Positive is fueled by her desire to provide a healing community that is lively and inspiring for her clients suffering with eating disorders. It is a community that offers freedom from suffocating societal messages that keep people in a perpetual struggle with their bodies. She has co-created within The Body Positive a culture of recovery and joy in which people find the courage to leave body hatred behind and turn their attention to fully inhabiting their lives.

. . .

Although the world has not changed in many of the ways I'd hoped when I made my commitment to Carmen so many years ago, her world became unique from the moment The Body Positive was founded. She grew up free to love and respect her physical self, which meant she didn't experience the fear (and in many cases hatred) most girls have of their growing, changing bodies. I didn't do this work alone; Carmen was immersed in a community of Body Positive individuals from the time she was four years old. She had as her role models people diverse in every way imaginable. Her babysitters were our teen peer leaders. She spent hours (probably more than she cared to!) standing by my side as I talked about my work to help people experience self-love and respect for their bodies.

Carmen is now grown and gone from home, and I see that the foundation she constructed growing up with The Body Positive serves her well. She is keenly aware of her physical needs and meets them as best she can. She is inoculated against the powerful influence of harmful messages about beauty and health. And, to my extreme delight, she uses her intuitive wisdom to guide not only her choices about physical self-care, but other life decisions as well.

My commitment to change the world for Carmen led to the creation of an organization where those who are ready to shift their beliefs about beauty, health, and identity in a positive direction are given the opportunity and resources to do so. I feel blessed to participate in the lives of so many courageous people who have chosen to defy status quo by making peace with their bodies and taking ownership of their lives. I am grateful that my suffering over my own body and the pain I experienced from the loss of my sister weren't in vain; it provided me with work I truly love and a way to make sense of what happened in my life.

NAMES AND VOICES

In reading *Embody*, you'll see The Body Positive name used in several different ways. "*The* Body Positive" is the name of our nonprofit organization. "*Be* Body Positive" is the name of the model we teach. And "Body Positive" is used as an adjective to describe the workshops and leadership trainings we conduct, the communities that are created by people who participate in our work, and the manner in which people choose to live in their bodies. For example, you'll read about Body Positive leaders, Body Positive communities, and people who are Body Positive.

As for the voices presented in *Embody*, I am the author and speak in the first person about my life. The ideas and teachings of The Body Positive, however, are both Elizabeth's and mine, so I use the plural pronouns "we," "our," and "us" to refer to the work she and I created together. "We" is also used in the universal sense as "we human beings who possess physical bodies."

I write this book from my perspective as a cisgender female, meaning I identify with the gender I was assigned at birth, which is female. I say this because my work has taught me the importance of stating out loud that my relationship with my body was formed because of my particular life circumstances and choices, and that I speak as the expert of *my body only*. I also write as a Caucasian, middle-aged, middle class woman who grew up in one particular part of the world. I do not pretend to know the experiences of others or what is "right" for anyone other than myself. I do know, however, that providing a safe space for people to be witnessed, whether others share the same particular story or not, is healing for both storyteller and listener.

ABOUT THIS BOOK AND HOW TO USE IT

"Stories matter. Many stories matter. Stories have been used to dispossess and to malign, but stories can also be used to empower and to humanize. Stories can break the dignity of a people, but stories can also repair that broken dignity."

—Chimamanda Adichie

Every one of us is living our own distinctive story—a body story, a heart story, a human story. Elizabeth and I are fortunate to spend time with a widely diverse group of people; our work is informed by every precious soul who has honored us by sharing their unique experience. We have made a commitment to telling our own stories, and offering space for others to do the same without fear of judgment, comparison, or criticism. It is in this type of environment that each one of us can find what we need to become embodied: to tell our own truth and step fully into— and love—our unique selves.

I've woven my own story of healing throughout the book; I've also included excerpts of my poetry, as well as anecdotes gathered from my work, relationships with others, and raising Carmen. Elizabeth's voice also appears throughout the text, adding her perspective as both a therapist and an individual who practices in her own life what she teaches to others. Short stories from an array of people who have had transformative experiences with The Body Positive are incorporated as well. You may relate to some of these stories, or not. What really matters is your own story. My hope is that the personal narratives provided will encourage you to uncover what's true for you.

. . .

Embody brings to life the five core Competencies of the Be Body Positive Model. In the "Welcome" you will find a brief overview of the model and how we use it. The next five chapters present the "Competencies" and are designed to give instruction as well as motivation for positive change. "What's Next" offers options for expanding your relationship to the concepts presented in this book.

At the end of each of the Competencies, you will find Body Positive Practices that provide practical ways to bring these concepts into your life. There is no "right" way to do them; they are offered to inspire you to think about what *you* need to enhance awareness and healing. Do the practices as they are presented, or change them to better suit your situation. As changes happen in your life you can even revisit them to gather more information. I do the practices whenever I facilitate a group, gathering new knowledge that enlightens my ever-changing relationship with my body and life. I save my writing, which I read every so often to reflect on the growth that has occurred over time.

Elizabeth and I do not promote a single end goal for success because the outcome of this exploration is as unique as every person who takes The Body Positive journey. We offer ourselves as guides along your path to making peace with your body. It is *your* voyage to be taken at whatever pace is right for *you*. Honor your individual rhythm and needs. The idea of loving and trusting your body may be completely new to you, or you may require only a few tools to move closer to knowing self-love on a daily basis. We respect wherever you are in your process and suggest that you take from *Embody* that which speaks to you in the moment.

Pick it up from time to time, or read it from cover to cover. Use your intuition to know what you need from the pages you read. Return to the book both as a reminder of your transformation and motivation for continued growth.

Welcome to The Body Positive!

"I attribute a great part of the healing I have done to The Body Positive. I was fortunate to have Connie and Elizabeth and a beautiful community of self-loving, respectful individuals at my doorstep when I needed them. The beauty of the Be Body Positive Model is that it's not just for women, or people with a diagnosed eating disorder. It is for men, women, mothers, fathers, brothers, sisters, and friends. It speaks to everyone with a body."

—Lily S., Body Positive leader

Welcome to the Body Positive

"In my 40+ pain-filled years of trying to survive life in an 'imper-fect' body, I've never run across a message that gave me so much hope. There is no possibility of failure here. There are no rules to follow or tests to pass before I am allowed to love my body—flaws and all—and choose to take care of myself because it feels good. The Body Positive offers compassion, humor, and a new brand of personal responsibility that comes from a place of love rather than fear."
—Kelle J., Body Positive workshop participant

Embody: Learning to Love Your Unique Body (and quiet that critical voice!) brings to life the work of The Body Positive, a nonprofit organization I co-created with Elizabeth Scott. I was introduced to Elizabeth in 1996 through mutual acquaintances who knew we were both interested in preventing eating disorders. Because she was a therapist specializing in this field, I asked her to facilitate a discussion with a group of teen girls for the promotional video I was producing to raise funds for my work.

Three monumental events happened as a result. The first was that the girls who came together for our day of videotaping did not want to end the conversation. They wanted to be an integral part of whatever The Body Positive would become. The second was that the bond Elizabeth and I formed led to our official partnership. Soon after we were introduced, it became evident that combining our skills would give us the power to make the changes we wished to see in the world. Then, in January of 1998, we received a grant that provided two years of funding for The Body Positive's first youth leadership program to prevent eating disorders.

Our work has since moved beyond this original focus. Yet at the core of *everything* we have developed is the "Be Body Positive Model," which provides people of *all* ages, sizes, sexual orientations, genders, ethnicities, abilities, and socioeconomic levels with a whole-person, non-shaming approach to the mystery and miracle of living in a human body.

The Be Body Positive Model is comprised of five core Competencies:

1. Reclaim Health
2. Practice Intuitive Self-Care
3. Cultivate Self-Love
4. Declare Your Own Authentic Beauty
5. Build Community

We call them core Competencies because they are the fundamental skills we practice on a daily basis to live peacefully and healthfully in our bodies. When we become proficient—*competent*—at using these skills, we are able to care for ourselves in body, mind, and spirit from a place of self-love and appreciation.

Through workshops, lectures, and leadership trainings, Elizabeth and I have worked intimately with thousands of people (primarily females, but an increasing number of males and transgender individuals) from young to old, and all ages in between. Our message has also reached millions of children, teens, and adults worldwide through the distribution of our peer-to-peer focused educational videos and curricula. We are delighted that it is now reaching you.

The Body Positive's philosophy is truly universal because it honors every person's unique knowledge and experience. The messages are straightforward and free of gimmicks. Rather than dictating a prescriptive set of rules to follow, we guide people through patient, mindful inquiry to find what works uniquely in their own lives to bring about positive self-care changes and a peaceful relationship with their bodies.

BECOMING YOUR OWN AUTHORITY

"You never change things by fighting the existing reality. To change something, build a new model that makes the beginning model obsolete."

—Buckminster Fuller

The Be Body Positive Model teaches you to become the expert— the *authority*—of your own body by first recognizing, and then trusting, its innate wisdom. Sue Monk Kidd offers my favorite definition of the word *authority* in her book *The Dance of the Dissident Daughter*: "to stand forth with power and dignity." Elizabeth and I believe this: we *all* have the right to live with dignity; we *all* possess the power to make good decisions about our unique bodies when we learn to listen closely to the information they provide in every moment. We understand that choosing this path is much easier with support, which is why we have dedicated our lives to helping people reconnect with their inborn ability to identify—and pursue—what they need in order to thrive.

We do not offer a step-by-step plan to follow from Point A (body dissatisfaction, dieting, obsession with weight and image) to Point B (self-love, intuitive self-care, freedom from obsession). Our work does not resemble typical diet, health, fitness, or other self-improvement programs that instruct clients to follow certain steps to the letter in order to arrive at a promised definition of success—where if someone "fails" it's considered their fault, not the failing of a set of strict rules that can be impossible to stick to over the long term, even when offered with the best of intentions.

Our model is complete; five core Competencies address *all* of the obstacles to healing that Elizabeth and I unearthed during decades of preventing and treating eating and body image problems. The following graph illustrates what the Be Body Positive Model *offers*—and what it *does not*.

The Be Body Positive Model		
Tools for a lifetime of exploration	vs.	A static goal-oriented view of life
A practical framework of self-inquiry	vs.	A step-by-step program
A whole-person health model	vs.	A weight loss program
A definition of health that is based on balanced self-care and self-love	vs.	An idealized external image of a "healthy" person
No double binds	vs.	Conflicting messages that leave people confused or frustrated
Attuned self-care	vs.	"Rules" about eating and exercise

A foundation of self-love and forgiveness	vs.	"Shoulds" and punishment
A celebration of diversity as beauty	vs.	A limited definition of "ideal" beauty
The development of positive communities	vs.	Connecting with others through negative self-talk

DEFINING SUCCESS

"To exist is to change, to change is to mature, to mature is to go on creating oneself endlessly."

—Henri Bergson

Elizabeth and I have created a framework for true success because we define it not as a static, end goal of perfection, but as a way of living that gives you permission to love, care for, and take pleasure in your body throughout your lifespan. Struggles will inevitably occur, especially during times of transition or imbalance. Using the Be Body Positive Model core Competencies, however, allows you to find what you need to live with as much self-love and balanced self-care as possible. Experiences of conflict and suffering become opportunities to learn what is required to further your growth so you can find greater contentment and peace. The ideas we offer are meant to evolve in conjunction with the changes that will happen throughout your life; what you discover will be unique to you and your individual circumstances.

In her psychotherapy practice, Elizabeth has honed the model to address the biggest hurdles faced by people struggling with eating disorders when working to make peace with their bodies,

embody

eating, and exercise. This has helped to fine-tune and improve our model's core Competencies by ensuring that they offer a solution to even the most difficult challenges her clients have brought to the recovery process. Even those individuals who start working with her after enduring years of eating disorders and acute self-loathing move towards healing quickly when they are introduced to these ideas.

The Be Body Positive Model offers a path to freedom wherever people may currently be along the spectrum: from slight dissatisfaction with their bodies (or "garden variety body hatred" as one of our youth leaders named it), to active weight loss behaviors, to eating and exercise problems that require clinical help for recovery. We do not believe in a hierarchy of suffering; everyone—no matter where they may be along the continuum—deserves support to improve their self-care. The work not only enhances physical self-care, but has also been shown to increase self-esteem and reduce anxiety and depression.

The five Competencies are basic "tools" we can use to contact our precious natural resources of trust, intuition, balance, and connection. They provide a structure free from judgment and blame that allows each of us—in our own individual way and time—to celebrate our physical bodies and (re)discover the beauty and self-love that are our birthright.

JESSICA DIAZ

THE BODY POSITIVE BOARD MEMBER

The Body Positive taught me that loving my body could transform my life. Nothing else has ever been so true! I can't control everything that happens to me. What I can control, however, is how I feel about myself. When life gets rough, I have the power to come back to a deep love for myself. I return to a trust that I have wisdom in my body, that I know what's right for me. I've tested out different ways of being with myself; I've learned that what works and what feels best is loving myself even through moments of struggle, even when it feels like I can't find any reason to keep going on. When life gets hard I try to reach down deep for what it is that I know, and what I know is it feels so much better to love myself. I want to share this knowledge with the world, because imagine all that you could achieve if you really tried on the idea that you could—no matter what life threw at you and what you went through—come home to a love for yourself.

PAYING ATTENTION TO THE POWER OF LANGUAGE

"Fat: This is the simplest word to describe people who are larger than average...The F-word is nothing to be afraid of! It holds no negative judgment, unless we put one there. We say young and old, short and tall, why can't we also say thin and fat?"
—Marilyn Wann, *Fat!So?*

At The Body Positive, we take great care to use respectful, empowering, and positive language when talking about weight. This is essential for reducing weight-based shame and honoring the genetic diversity of human shapes and sizes. We do not presume that a fat person is unhealthy, nor do we assume that a thin person is healthy, or that an extremely thin person has an eating disorder.

We find it useful to talk about *natural*, or *set-point*, weight— the size each individual is genetically programmed to maintain within a certain range. We use the word *fat* without judgment to describe a fat person. We say *fat* with the same energy as we say other physical descriptors, such as *thin, tall, short, brown eyed,* or *curly haired.*

We do not use the words *overweight* or *obese* unless we are describing how society views people in these terms, and then we use them in quotation marks (as you'll notice throughout this book). We cannot consider someone to be "overweight" by looking at them, because we don't *know* their genetically-determined weight, or whether or not they are "over" that weight. We don't use the word "obese" because, in our opinion, it has become a word used to judge and shame people instead of simply to describe a size.

We also do not use euphemistic words like *big boned* or *voluptuous,* for they imply that we shouldn't say the word *fat* because it is considered a "bad" word. The Body Positive is part of the size pride movement that is reclaiming the word *fat* as a neutral descriptor of a person's body type. It is a movement comprised of people of *all* sizes who understand the harm caused by weight stigma and messages linking weight to health, beauty, and self-worth.

Sometimes people who live in bodies that could be described as fat say they do not like the word, even those who regard themselves as size-acceptance activists. The word fat has been used to harm them too many times, so they use different words. Others, whose bodies could be considered thin or skinny, express dislike of *these* types of words, having also been harassed about their size by being accused of having anorexia or bulimia.

It is up to every person (of any size) to be sensitive to the power of language regarding weight and to choose defining words that are respectful of self and others. The easiest way to achieve this goal is to refrain from making assumptions about anyone's health or lifestyle based solely on appearance, and by relating to one another as whole beings, not body sizes.

USING THE BE BODY POSITIVE MODEL IN YOUR OWN LIFE

"The Be Body Positive Model works because it's not built on being satisfied with your body for just one day or even a week. It gives you the foundation to love and honor your body for the rest of your life."

—Caelayn B., Body Positive leader

The Be Body Positive model shifts the focus from attempting to "fix what's wrong" with your body to a practice of improving and maintaining self-care behaviors that are motivated by positive rather than punishing forces. The Competencies are offered over the next five chapters in a particular order because they build upon one another. As you integrate them into your daily life, however, you will discover that each is part of a whole process and the order becomes irrelevant. You address whatever particular issue arises in the moment with your new skills.

As you practice the Competencies, you cultivate the art of forgiveness for making "mistakes" with food, exercise, and other life choices, and allow yourself to learn and grow from your daily experiences. Over time you relax into the trial and error process of learning to eat and move—and live—intuitively. As your definition of beauty expands, you have the extraordinary opportunity to see beauty everywhere, *starting with yourself.* You may develop friendships with people who also choose to appreciate their own bodies, and enter into (or stay in) relationships *only* with those who love and respect yours, just as it is in the moment. When the inevitable burdens that come with being human start to weigh you down, you have your Body Positive community for support, as well as the ability to employ humor and self-love to lighten the load when you are alone.

ELIZABETH

FREEDOM FROM DOUBLE BINDS

---

double bind, (*noun*): a situation in which a person is confronted with two irreconcilable demands or a choice between two undesirable courses of action [1]

Connie and I consciously created The Body Positive's messages to avoid causing double binds. A double bind happens when we are put into a conflict between two opposing pieces of information. For example, we are told being thin will make us happy. It may, however, be genetically impossible for some of us to lose weight and keep it off, so we end up unhappier than before we attempted weight loss. Or we are already thin (or get thin through restricting our food and/or over-exercising), but still have problems that make us unhappy.

Another example of a double bind is being told that embracing a spiritual life will lead to weight loss. Finding spirituality is a wonderful achievement, but it won't necessarily lead to weight loss. Some people may lose weight when they pay attention to their spiritual needs, some won't. It doesn't make a person any less spiritual if they don't drop a clothing size.

An extremely harmful double bind is the message that we must lose weight to become healthy. Since we know that restrictive dieting can lead to weight regain and worsened health (especially if the pattern is repeated again and again or an eating disorder develops), this message is seriously dangerous.

If your natural body does not fit the societal ideal, you can get lost by endlessly trying to transform yourself into a shape or size that goes against your genetic inheritance. Nothing good comes of this dead-end pursuit, which more often than not leads to feelings of frustration and despair. If your goal is to lose enough weight so you'll be loved, or free from reproach or criticism, you'll get stuck in a double bind. The world is full of aggression. Even if you achieve a socially prescribed ideal weight and image, you are still faced with being a mere mortal and life's inevitable problems.

The Be Body Positive Model teaches people to expand their resources to become better equipped to face life's difficulties. We help them to first recognize, then step away from, the double-binding messages they receive from family, friends, and the world at large.

I encourage you to notice the double binds embedded in the messages you read in books or hear from family, friends, medical professionals, media, etc. You may find some parts of what you are being told very useful. Other suggestions from the same source, however, might not make any sense to you because they contradict what has previously been conveyed. A good way to recognize when you're confronted with a double bind is to notice what signals your body gives you. I notice a sick feeling in my stomach, as if I can't "digest" the idea being presented. What do you notice? Over time you will learn to recognize double binds and have the ability to take in only the information that feels right for your unique body and life.

It takes practice and conscious awareness to experience life through a Body Positive lens. After time, however, you'll realize you've embodied the Competencies, because it feels natural to care for yourself from a place of kindness and trust. When you become attuned to your intuition, you begin to move towards experiences and people that feel healthy on an intrinsic level. As one leader said at a community dinner, "It's a process to take this all in, but once you do, it just becomes part of your everyday life. It's addictive!" The addiction spoken of here is the commitment to self-love, the ability to see great beauty in one's self as well as in others, and the pursuit of positive, joyful self-care. What could be better?

Please remember, as with all things "worth their weight," changing your relationship with your body can be messy and painful at times. It takes practice. But Elizabeth and I believe this journey is worth every ounce of energy you put into it. Getting to the place where you are free to live without restriction, where your fears and self-criticism lessen in intensity because your voice of kindness and compassion grows in strength each day, *feels good*. Communication becomes easier when you can express your true thoughts and feelings because the practice of self-love protects you from taking in judgment—or helps you quickly release any negativity that does get under your skin. Beauty surrounds you in abundance and life becomes a richer, more meaningful experience.

"Embodying the Be Body Positive Model's core Competencies is simple and it's not. It's choosing love as often as we can. It's finding humor when we look at the imagery society offers up as beauty. It's listening closely to our bodies and doing our best to follow their wisdom. It's forgiving ourselves when we make 'mistakes.' Ultimately, it's honoring our bodies in all their varied forms as precious and worthy of love and respect."
—Lisa E., Body Positive workshop participant

COMPETENCY ONE

Reclaim Health

···

GOALS

- Uncover the messages that have influenced your relationships with your body, food, and exercise.
- Develop a weight-neutral, health-centered approach to self-care.

BENEFIT

Become the authority of your own body by sorting out facts from distorted societal myths about health, weight, and identity.

···

"We need to restore some sensibility to the pursuit of health. Many of us increasingly view ourselves as fragile and vulnerable, ready to develop cancer, heart disease, or some other dreaded disease at the slightest provocation. In the name of health we give up many of our enjoyments. The important point is that worrying too much about anything—be it calories, salt, cancer, or cholesterol—is bad for you, and that living optimistically, with pleasure, zest, and commitment, is good."

—Robert Ornstein, PhD, David Sobel, MD, *Healthy Pleasures*

Reclaim Health, the first Competency of the Be Body Positive Model, explores health from a weight-neutral, pleasure-focused position that is grounded in the study of human physiology. Extensive research supports the argument that measurements of physical activity and metabolic fitness, such as blood pressure, blood lipids, and blood sugar levels, are far better indicators of physical health than body size.[1] This allows us to move away from moralistic, judgmental views of weight towards a whole-person approach—based on sound evidence—that values a positive relationship with one's body and long term, stable, self-care behaviors as primary to physical wellbeing.

Reclaiming your health is an opportunity to become the authority of your own body. This does not mean you rule over it and attempt to beat it into submission. Rather, you treat it with respect by listening to its wisdom so you know what you need in order to thrive. You are empowered to act in accordance with this innate knowledge, even if it means living outside of society's expectations of what a healthy person looks like. *YOU are the ultimate expert of your body.*

OBSTACLES TO ACHIEVING BALANCED, SUSTAINABLE SELF-CARE

Balanced, sustainable eating and exercise habits are fundamental to achieving the best possible health for our particular genetics and life circumstances, so we must be watchful for any obstacles that might get in the way. One such obstacle is the current societal belief system linking health to size. Most people think that to be healthy one must be thin, or conversely, that thin people are in good physical shape simply because of their size. This association falsely implies that being fat is inherently harmful and sends the message to slender people that they don't have to think much about their self-care habits.

We are bombarded with messages that support this view. How many times each day are you told, from one source or another, that fat is bad and thinness is what you should be thinking about, striving for, and pursuing with fervor at all times? The weight loss industry (or *weight cycling* industry, as psychologist and author Deb Burgard, PhD calls it) generates about $60 billion in annual sales.[2] Equating thinness with health is in the best financial interest of the companies involved.

HOW DO YOU DEFINE HEALTH?

Health is a dynamic concept, informed and constructed by both society and science. As such, it is useful to pause and consider your personal definition. Ask yourself: *How do I define health? What do I think a healthy person looks like? How did I develop these beliefs?* You might find it helpful to jot down your answers to these questions and explore them as you read this chapter.

The Famine Response

"...being pleasantly plump is healthier than subjecting ourselves to the ups and downs of constant dieting. And while there is no question that what and how we eat is related to our health, 'dieting' is not a healthy way to eat."
—Robert Ornstein, PhD, David Sobel, MD, *Healthy Pleasures*

You've probably heard diets don't work, but it is hard to believe if all you see in the media is an emphasis on thinness and the glorification of anyone who accomplishes this goal. Apparently, we

41

should all be able to lose weight and keep it off with will power and self-discipline. That's what the companies selling us their products and services want us to believe. Why, then, do most people on restrictive diets regain the pounds they lose—and often more?

The answer lies in the physiology of the human body, which is genetically programmed to hold on to weight for evolutionary reasons having to do with survival. Those of our ancestors who both stored fat easily and slowed energy output were most protected during times of famine, when the cells of the body use as little energy as possible to maximize efficiency and conserve precious calories. This function is called the "famine response."

In effect, the body cannot recognize the difference between a diet and a famine. So when we go on a restrictive diet, our energy-regulating systems slow down in order to conserve every bit of fuel that comes in. This physiological response—one that actively stores more food as fat in the body during times of under-nourishment—is specifically designed to help us survive.

Every calorie-restrictive diet triggers the famine response because the body senses a state of starvation. But, when the diet ends and former eating habits resume, *the body continues to conserve energy*; it takes fewer calories to put the weight back on, and often more is added.[3] In other words, *the more we diet, the easier it is to gain weight*! Furthermore, this cycling pattern (yo-yo dieting) makes it increasingly difficult to lose weight with every subsequent diet given that cells are programmed to hold on to every calorie possible in order to successfully survive what seem like frequent famines.[4]

Diet Programs: A Set Up for Failure

"When I was dieting, food would talk to me…like those cookies on top of the refrigerator, they would sound out my name!"
    —Lisa T., The Body Positive advisory board member

I meet a lot of people who tell me they've been on a weight loss program their whole lives and believe it's been a useful way to help them "control" their weight. When I probe a bit, I usually discover that they haven't been *on* the program their whole lives, they've been on—and off—and their weight has gone down and up accordingly.

I understand the draw of programs that promise weight loss, especially ones that offer group support for their members. I believe it is the support of the community that keeps people going back. Their primary problem, however, is that the behaviors they teach, like counting points or calories and avoiding certain food groups, don't *sustain* long-term weight stability for the majority of their customers. That means they set people up to fail. Focusing on the number on the scale as the ultimate measure of success leads many to quit if they don't lose weight fast enough, or if their bodies won't let them reach an unrealistic goal for their heredity or age. Unfortunately, any positive changes are lost in the process.

KIM HOWELL

BODY POSITIVE LEADERSHIP TRAINING PARTICIPANT

"Every opinion based on scientific criticism, I welcome. As to the prejudices of so-called public opinion, to which I have never made concessions, now as aforetime the maxim of the great Florentine is mine: Segui il tuo corso, e lascia dir le genti—*Follow your own road, and let the people talk."* —KARL MARX

The above quotation is one of my most beloved. Not only does quoting Karl Marx tend to raise eyebrows, but the notion of following one's own road without concessions or consideration of public opinion can also be viewed as rather unconventional. But that's me—unconventional.

Growing up in a midwestern, upper-middle class neighborhood, a more keen focus was placed on my race than my weight. I spent a great deal of time feeling different because of the color of my skin, but not the size of my body. Fast forward a couple of decades—I moved from Ohio to Southern California. I was tossed into a world of people from a host of countries, a multitude of textures, races, and ethnicities. No sooner had I begun to feel at home with my race, than something else reared its ugly head—the impression that my weight and size now made me unconventional, and not in a good way. I was surrounded by people who engaged in procedures to change parts of their bodies I had no idea could be manipulated—and these were people I loved and admired! I was in a community of people I found stunningly beautiful who spent hours on end picking apart their every perceived "flaw." I too began to see my flaws, and I fell into a downward spiral of disordered eating and living. I was miserable.

During this time, I was seeing a psychiatrist who said to me, "Your problem is that you do have an eating disorder, but you also have a high Body Mass Index, so you're going to need to lose weight. I suggest you do it in a safe, healthy environment." So, I joined Weight Watchers with my sister, and soon we both became obsessed scale junkies, doomed to find our worthiness in a number.

Ironically, during this process I decided to use my disordered eating as the driving force behind my doctoral dissertation, which led me to my first Body Positive workshop In October 2011. It changed my life. I showed up with my little brown bag of breakfast and lunch items with an awareness of each and every precious Weight Watcher point encased within. But then something happened...I found myself surrounded by young people seeking more knowledge of how to spread the word of self-love and acceptance across their high school and college campuses, and I was moved. These exquisite people were all shapes, sizes, ages, genders, and nationalities—a pure amalgamation of beauty. I could not shake how wonderful it felt to be accepted just as I was in the present moment.

During that magical weekend, I embarked upon a new relationship with food as well as my body. I learned to listen to my body; I learned to respect food. I discovered that my body knows what and how much I need if I merely stop, breathe, and allow it its much deserved respect and adoration. I called my sister from the workshop and said, "Well, it's a long story, but not only am I not going back to Weight Watchers, I'd love it if you could get rid of my scale before I get home because I'm never stepping on it again."

My sister and I now engage in intuitive eating practices and encourage one another to love ourselves, just as we are. I am making strides with my own body story and continue to empower others to love themselves and each other. The world would be such a boring place if everyone looked the same, so I now work to help others see how glorious our communities are with the diversity of human shapes and sizes. "*Segui il tuo corso, e lascia dir le genti*—Follow your own road, and let the people talk."

The Simplistic and Misleading
Body Mass Index

"What I've learned the hard way is that the BMI tells you nothing about a patient's health."

—Toni Martin, MD

Body Mass Index (BMI), a well-known and widely used measure of health, divides individuals into categories of "underweight," "optimal weight," "overweight," and "obese" based simply upon a rather meaningless calculation of a height-to-weight ratio. Why do I say meaningless? Let's take a look at the creation of the BMI and how it came to be used as a measure of health, as shared by author J. Eric Oliver in his book *Fat Politics* and summarized below.

Belgian astronomer Adolphe Quetelet invented the BMI calculation in the 1830s because he was interested in observing "norms" in human beings as determined by the bell curve. The measurement had nothing to do with body fat, mortality, or disease, and more to do with the mathematical laws of probability.

In the 1940s, the Metropolitan Life Insurance Company adopted the BMI measurement to determine how much to charge their customers for insurance. Without any scientifically determined evidence showing a causal link between weight and health, they came up with "ideal" weight charts. Soon after, thanks to forceful lobbying by one of the Metropolitan Life statisticians, this misleading measurement was adopted by doctors, epidemiologists, and the U.S. government as a way to determine the health of the American population.[5]

The history of the BMI reveals that it is actually a poor indicator of *anyone's* health! The fact that it does not account or control for variables such as gender, age, race, and cultural background also supports this revelation. Furthermore, the BMI does not distinguish between weight originating from fat tissue versus weight originating from muscle tissue. It is simply a measure of how much an individual's body type varies from the weight/height ratio "norm" found in human beings.

To make matters worse, a panel of specialists brought together in 1998 by the National Health, Lung, and Blood Institute lowered the BMI numbers for all weight categories. Overnight, people who were once considered to be in the "optimal weight" range became "overweight," and those who were "overweight" became "obese." Studies done in recent years show that much of the hype over the "obesity epidemic" has been based on false information. In fact, researchers at the Centers for Disease Control found that people categorized as slightly "overweight" per their BMI have *lower* mortality rates than people in other categories, including the "optimal weight" category.[6]

These findings support The Body Positive's preference to define health *without including BMI*.

A War Against Fat Has Been Declared— and it's Harmful

"If [diets] really worked, we'd be running out of dieters."
—Glenn Gaesser, PhD, author of *Big Fat Lies: The Truth about Your Weight and Your Health*

The United States and many other countries have declared a war on fat. Former U.S. Surgeon General Dr. C. Everett Koop created his program *Shape Up America!* as a "great crusade" to combat "obesity." It is worth noting that funding for *Shape Up America!* came from Weight Watchers, Jenny Craig, and Slimfast, among others.[7] A subsequent U.S. Surgeon General, Richard Carmona, went so far as to label "obesity" as a "terror within," stating that it is "every bit as threatening to us as is the terrorist threat we face today."[8] While many public health programs emphasize healthy eating and exercise habits, they also frighten people by using "obesity prevention" language, which generally leads to short-term changes in weight and lifestyle only.[9] What's more, there is growing concern among medical and mental health practitioners that these "war on obesity" messages are causing preoccupation with food, weight loss/weight gain cycling, eating disorders, weight stigmatization, and other physical and mental health issues.[10]

Sizeism: A Consequence of the War Against Fat

"That one size we are hoping to reach—the size at which we will be safe from abandonment, rejection, and disintegration—is only an illusion. That size can never be reached, and if we constantly strive to obtain it, it will never be found. Protection from suffering does not come from a number on a scale, a size in one's clothing, or an approving look from another. Freedom can only be found when you hear your voice and have the courage to follow it."
—Alyssa B., Body Positive leader

The hysteria related to health and weight promotes fear and shame for people of all sizes; no one wants to experience the discrimination and harassment fat people encounter on a daily basis. "Sizeism" (or "weightism," as it is sometimes labeled) has developed into a socially acceptable form of oppression. The prevalence of discrimination based on body size is now close to the prevalence of gender or race bias, and in some situations even higher.[11] Studies show that health professionals (even those who are "obesity" specialists) treat their larger patients with less sensitivity, patience, and respect than smaller individuals.[12] Numerous people have had health services or insurance denied to them because of their size.[13] Additionally, women, people of color, and those living at lower socioeconomic levels are statistically more likely to be fat, linking size discrimination to social bigotry and other inequities.[14]

On the other hand, people who are exceptionally thin also face teasing and discrimination, the assumption being that such a low weight could only be the result of an eating disorder. The media attack Hollywood stars for putting on weight, but when those same celebrities respond by taking it off, they are once again a cover story. As the voyeuristic audience, we are supposed to be appalled by their weight gain and then horrified if they develop an eating disorder. The line between fat and thin is a fickle one.

I once had an encounter on an airplane that offers a reminder of what can be gained when we see people as whole human beings, and what is lost if we succumb to prejudice. I was flying home from San Diego, where I had been working at a high school with a group of Body Positive leaders. The students had conducted a weeklong body image event on campus that culminated with an extremely powerful play created by their theater department.

I was so emotionally high on the flight home that I could have fueled the airplane with my energy alone! Being the last person to board, only middle seats were available. I plopped my bag down on a seat near the rear of the plane and went to the bathroom. On my way out of the stall, a flight attendant approached me and said, "I'm so sorry you have to sit next to that man. We'll see what we can do to help you out." I was immediately offended by his disparaging words, because I knew he was talking about my seatmate who happened to be fat.

"Excuse me?" I asked, "I don't understand what you're talking about." (I knew exactly what he meant, but wanted to hear what would come next.)

"We'll send someone back here to give you a partial refund of your ticket since you're being inconvenienced by sitting next to *him*," said the flight attendant, glancing up the aisle.

I put my hands on my hips, said in a loud and indignant voice, "I'm fine, thank you very much!" and walked away. Throughout this interaction, my seatmate had been standing up awaiting my return; it was evident he had overheard the whole exchange. As soon as I sat down, I told him with enthusiasm about my experience watching the play. I explained The Body Positive's work, including our position on weight and health. The flight ended up being the most interesting I've ever had.

This man was extremely calm and thoughtful, especially compared to my jazzed up state. While I talked a mile a minute, he interjected simple yet profound statements that I could feel were expanding my understanding of what I was experiencing in my life and work at that particular time. He told me he had been a sound healer for many years and explained the way he used different instruments to physically and emotionally cure people. As he spoke, I could hear in my head and feel throughout my body the sound he would choose to help me become more centered and grounded. It's hard to explain, but I could literally feel his healing of me happening right then and there, without even having an instrument involved. We didn't speak about what he was thinking or what was going on for me. But something definitely happened on an energetic level, and I was left with a deep sense of faith in myself.

Throughout the previous year, I had been struggling with this very issue: how to trust my intuition to know what was required for the growth of The Body Positive. In the months that followed that flight home from San Diego, my voice became strong and I was able to clearly articulate what I truly felt was needed. I attribute this action directly to the clarity I gained from my short time with the beautiful man on the airplane. Had I only seen him as "taking up space," I never would have received the profound wisdom he offered me with his straightforward words and gifts as a sound healer.

Bariatric Surgery:
A Dangerous "Cure for Obesity"

Many people are now attempting weight loss through bariatric surgery, a procedure that restricts the amount of food that can be eaten and digested. This course of action is purported to be a "cure for obesity," but it is important to understand the risks involved.

In *Health at Every Size: The Surprising Truth About Your Weight,* author Linda Bacon, PhD, lists myriad complications including— to name just a few—dumping (abdominal cramps, bloating, palpitations, nausea, vomiting, diarrhea, and shortness of breath), bowel/fecal impaction, irregular body fat distribution (lumpy body), suicidal thoughts, weight regain, and risk for the development of anorexia or bulimia. Dr. Bacon cites studies showing that up to 15 percent of these patients die over a seven-to-nine year post-surgery period.[15] For older adults, the death rate within the first year after surgery has been shown to be up to 50 percent.[16] How disturbing that these procedures continue to be promoted in the name of health improvement, even with the associated complications and high mortality rate.

ELIZABETH

WHEN IS BARIATRIC SURGERY A "SUCCESS?"

I am troubled by the idea of bariatric surgery as a "cure for obesity" because it reminds me of an upsetting encounter I once had with a woman at a conference. I was teaching the group about the Be Body Positive Model, and as I talked about dieting, weight cycling, and bariatric surgeries, I mentioned

---

how sad I feel that people are constantly fighting their natural body size, willing to endure so much suffering in their efforts to become thin.

At the end of my lecture a woman came up to me and told me she had been through a "successful" bariatric surgery, because she had lost a substantial amount of weight. She felt so good about herself that she signed papers to allow her fourteen-year-old daughter to receive the same procedure. This girl had the surgery, lost weight, and died six months later. The mother was profoundly distressed, and deeply damaged by her participation in allowing the operation to be done on her young daughter. These surgeries can kill people who would not have died otherwise—people who could have lived healthy, peaceful lives in fat bodies.

In order to undergo bariatric surgery, or allow a child to do so, one has to believe that thinness is worth dying for. I see this in clients with eating disorders and fight it every day in my therapy practice. I'm constantly overwhelmed by sadness and grief for these precious individuals who are harming themselves in a multitude of ways because of their problematic relationships with their bodies. I'm furious with a society that promotes and glamorizes the behaviors that are killing them. The cost is extremely high.

ETHICAL CONSIDERATIONS

One highly alarming aspect of our society's devotion to dieting is the unethical relationship between the diet industry and medical research. As Pat Lyons, RN, MA, reveals in her chapter, "Prescription for Harm," in *The Fat Studies Reader*, strategies for "obesity" research, treatment, and prevention are being driven by the profits of the weight-loss industry. The same "obesity experts" who make huge profits running weight loss clinics also serve as faculty of medical institutions and National Institutes of Health (NIH) panelists that define public health priorities. As Ms. Lyons points out, these supposedly unbiased "experts" obtain millions of dollars in NIH research grants and review research papers for publication in medical journals, while simultaneously maintaining relationships as paid consultants and board members of weight loss and pharmaceutical companies.[17]

In contrast to the amount of money being spent to "cure obesity," relatively little is being done to treat the rapidly escalating number of people suffering from severely poor body image, yo-yo dieting, and dangerous eating disorders that have stemmed from the nation's hysteria surrounding weight. The number of people hospitalized for eating disorders has risen dramatically since 1999,[18] as have the costs. Individuals and families pay an average of $30,000 per month for inpatient or residential treatment with little help from their insurance companies.[19] Inpatient care generally lasts from three to six months.[20]

We think it is cruel and unethical to promote or prescribe weight loss through restrictive dieting, pills, or surgery. This is especially true when considering the scientific evidence proving these interventions are rarely effective long term—and quite often unsafe or even lethal.

JESSICA DIAZ

THE BODY POSITIVE BOARD MEMBER

I once went to my HMO for an appointment about a rash I had on my arm. The nurse who was seeing me that day came in, checked me up and down, and launched into a physical activity

---

assessment. I mentioned that I take dance classes and swim several times per week. She looked at me from above her glasses and said, "I'm sure you know you should lose weight."

I held her stare and replied, "I'm not here to talk about my weight."

She ignored me and said, "Well, I am instructed to talk about weight loss with people who have high blood pressure."

I asked, "Can you please check my chart to see if I have high blood pressure?" She looked through my chart and grimaced. "Do I have high blood pressure?" I repeated.

She replied, "No, you are perfectly healthy."

"Great," I said. "Now let's talk about why I'm here."

HEALTH: BODY POSITIVE STYLE

"Reexamine all you have been told in school or church or in any book, and dismiss whatever insults your own soul; and your very flesh shall be a great poem, and have the richest fluency, not only in words, but in the silent lines of its lips and face and between the lashes of your eyes, and in every motion and joint of your body."
—Walt Whitman, *Leaves of Grass*

We take a giant step towards giving our bodies what they need to thrive when we move away from the belief that health comes in a certain size, or that it is a state of perfection that can be attained (and sustained) by attempts to rigidly control our eating and exercise. Viewing health from a whole-person perspective allows us to create a lifestyle that meets our needs on all levels—physical, emotional, mental, and spiritual.

Being healthy in Body Positive terminology means inhabiting your body fully. Life circumstances (e.g., injuries, illnesses, disabilities, time constraints, and levels of access to nutritious foods and safe places to exercise) may affect your capacity to maintain consistent self-care; all that is required is to do the best you can, taking into consideration your situation in the moment.

Delight in all the things your body *can* do and take pleasure in using it, whenever possible. Use pain and discomfort as signals that adjustments may be needed, and take action to make the changes that are within your power. Thank your body when it is working well, and give it love and forgiveness when it is not.

The Body Positive definition of health expands beyond the physical to include care for emotional and spiritual needs as well. Reach for kindness and compassion when you are faced with difficult life experiences, and use moments of struggle as opportunities for growth rather than punishment. Self-love is the ultimate source for making life easier—it leads to better self-care on all levels.

In Body Positive workshops we gather participants together in small groups to discuss what health means to them and how to define it in ways they can easily communicate to others. Here is a definition from one of these groups that summarizes what we hear most often.

Health is:

- A holistic view of a person's life

- More than just physical wellness

- Being able to cope with emotions and life experiences in a positive way, whenever possible

- Seeking balance in ALL areas of life (physical, mental, spiritual, emotional)

- Making decisions determined by one's own motivation for doing things (e.g., moving to feel good rather than to lose weight as one might be told to do by a fitness program)

- Being sensible (for the most part!)

- Keeping an open mind

- Not obsessing over food and weight

- Having prospering relationships

- Being comfortable in one's skin

- Living life in a purposeful, beneficial manner

Become Your Own Health Expert

"When we rely on authorities to tell us what we need, we have little ability to filter these messages and pressures. If we become our own authorities, we can learn what's right for us. We can take in information and say, 'No, this isn't for me, or maybe, 'Yes, this feels right.' With this ability, we find our balance. What's so beautifully simple is that we each possess this wisdom already. It's not something we must struggle to learn, but rather a process of peeling back the layers to see how we may have lost it in order to find it again."

—Sammy Jo R., Body Positive leader

To become your own expert, it is critical to examine the messages you've received—and continue to receive—throughout your life about health, weight, food, and exercise (also beauty, but we'll get to that in a later chapter). You'll want to pay attention not only to what you've been told by the media and medical professionals, but also by your family, friends, and culture.

Once you clearly identify the messages, you can begin to think critically about which ones work for you. If particular information is intriguing, try it out to see how it makes you feel. If you adopt a behavior that leads to better physical and/or mental health, and—most importantly—it is something you can sustain over the long term, keep it in your toolkit. From this same observant position, you can also identify the messages that trigger guilt or shame. If the information *doesn't* make you feel better or is a behavior you can't maintain over time, discard it and return to what you know to be right for you.

I want to be clear that I'm *not* telling you to ignore what your doctor or other health practitioners tell you. For example, if a physician says your blood pressure or cholesterol level is high, you'll want to pay attention and take action. If you are instructed to take medication for either of these conditions (or others), you will want to listen to your intuition to see if that feels like the right course of action. What you don't want to do is follow the advice of an "expert" blindly, especially if they tell you it's imperative that you lose weight to improve your health—and suggest going on a diet. Perhaps your condition will improve by increasing physical activity or making dietary and other life changes. Or, you may feel it's right to take the medication. It is up to you to listen to the signals from within to help with these kinds of decisions.

Let me repeat: even with information from "experts," it is vitally important to conduct a personal experiment to find out if specific advice is appropriate for you. Health messages come and go. Your body will know what works best for you; your job is to listen and respond accordingly. Over time, as you get more closely in touch with your intuitive wisdom, you'll be able to more easily discern how best to care for your unique body.

The following story illustrates how my experimentation process lets me be my own expert and care for myself in the best way possible.

Kale. One day it seemed that everywhere I went, people were raving about the health benefits of kale. Though I'd always loved leafy greens, kale wasn't one I sought out. People told me how much they liked sautéed kale, kale chips, and other kale recipes, so I thought I'd give it a shot. But, try as I might, I couldn't make myself like it. Cooked? Yuck! Raw? Scary! I continued to purchase big bunches of the beautiful green vegetable, even though guilt consumed me each time I dumped it—wilted and rotting—into my compost bin. Finally, I accepted the fact that I didn't like kale and stopped pretending I would make myself eat it, even if "experts" said it would enhance my health.

When a new friend gave me a salad recipe that sounded intriguing, I decided to give it one more chance. The recipe was fun to create (the dressing and other ingredients were massaged into the kale by hand!), and the final product was aesthetically pleasing, filling my big bamboo bowl with vibrant color and a perfect combination of flavors and textures.

Suddenly, I craved kale salad. I added it to my eggs in the morning, and ate it as a side or main dish for lunch and dinner. I made the salad for all of my friends, and talked about it like it was a new lover. When purchasing kale in the market, people would make comments about how "good" I was being and that they knew they "should" eat it. I, of course, had to tell my story about how much I actually hated this particular vegetable until I discovered the salad, which led to people pulling out scraps of paper and shopping lists to quickly scribble the recipe down before I left the store.

After several weeks of eating the kale salad regularly, I noticed my digestive system was hyperactive and that I was spending an inordinate amount of time in the bathroom. It quickly became obvious that kale was something my body only needed in small amounts. Though I had heard eating it in abundance was "good" for me, obviously, for *my* body, it wasn't.

As you can see from this story, it was more important for me to listen to my body than to outside recommendations about the health benefits of eating large quantities of kale. I learned new information, conducted my own personal experiment to test it out, and honored the results by adjusting the amount of kale I consumed.

We become experts when we are willing to conduct experiments like these and respond to the information we gather. If your eating and exercise habits seem appropriate for your lifestyle and you are happy with the state of your health, continue with what feels right. If you want to make changes in your self-care routine and are intrigued by what you read or hear, pay close attention to how your body responds as you carry out your research. Over time, you build trust in your ability to recognize your unique requirements for food, movement, rest, pleasure, and social support, allowing you to live as healthfully as possible—given your genetics and current life circumstances.

True Pleasure Leads to Healthy Choices

"Good health is much closer to home, much simpler (and more enjoyable) than we imagined. It derives from a pursuit of healthy pleasures. ... In short, the healthiest people seem to be pleasure-loving, pleasure-seeking, pleasure-creating individuals."
—Robert Ornstein, PhD, David Sobel, MD, *Healthy Pleasures*

I am incredibly sad that pleasure has gotten a bad rap in the health world. Approaching health as a moral duty can cause people to fail in achieving their physical goals, because the process becomes a chore with unreasonably high expectations. Think about how many people's primary New Year's resolution is to lose weight by dieting and exercising every day. As we know, these newly adopted relationships with food and exercise often slip away quickly because the motivation behind them is about weight loss and being "good" rather than making lifestyle changes that are fun and sustainable.

When we focus on *pleasurable* self-care we have a much better chance of maintaining good health. As Sobel and Ornstein discuss in their book *Healthy Pleasures*, it is in our genetic coding to engage in pleasurable behaviors because this gave us a greater chance of survival as we evolved as a species. The enjoyable activities and flavors pursued by our early ancestors were the ones that kept them alive.[21]

One of the problems people have with the concept of pleasure is its association with excess and being "bad," which is how they describe the experience of breaking dieting rules, letting go of control, giving in to vices, etc., as in, "I was *bad* yesterday because I ate a pint of ice cream." When I was bulimic, I thought bingeing gave me pleasure, because during the time I let myself eat whatever I wanted in large quantities I was free from my restrictive diet. It was my rebellion against the part of me that was rigid and afraid. I wanted to be "bad" to thwart my jail keeper's plans to keep me contained.

I admit, the first few bites of a binge gave me great pleasure because of the freedom I felt, but eating far beyond physical fullness only brought pain and suffering. The aftereffect resembled nothing even close to freedom; I felt utterly trapped in my obsession. When I learned (over time and with much practice!) that it was extraordinarily pleasurable to savor the food I chose to eat and to stop when I felt physically satisfied, I no longer needed to eat to the point of feeling sick and disgusted with myself. I was able to experience this new way of eating *only when I gave myself permission to have—and enjoy—any foods I wanted at any time.*

You may (or may not) be familiar with the mantra of most dieters: *Tomorrow, I'll begin my diet. This is the last time I'll eat this food, so I'll eat as much of it as possible right now since I'll never have it again. Tomorrow, I'll be good. I promise!*

I became free from this distorted practice only by ending my ban on "bad" foods. My new way of relating to food allowed me to satisfy a much deeper, intrinsic need that was motivated by the desire for *true* pleasure. This led to the creation of a self-care practice where I get immense enjoyment from eating all types of foods in moderate amounts and moving my body for enjoyment as well as fitness.

Moderation in All Things—
Including Excess

"Excess on occasion is exhilarating. It prevents moderation from acquiring the deadening effect of a habit."
—W. Somerset Maugham

The phrase I coined to help me maintain balance in my life is, "Moderation in all things—including excess." I sometimes eat beyond physical fullness because my taste buds delight in the flavors of my meal, and upon occasion I may drink a bit more than my body wants. When I'm on vacation in the Sierra Nevada mountains I tend to push my physical limits because I'm thrilled to be out in nature, and my soul gets fed by climbing granite mountains. From time to time I watch TV in excess because I'm sick or want to zone out, but, in general, I live in moderation. The beauty is this: moderation comes easily because I have given myself permission to have and do what I desire, and because I don't consider myself "bad" when I indulge in excess every so often.

When we "restore some sensibility to the pursuit of health," as Sobel and Ornstein suggest, we honor the gray areas of life. We move away from good/bad, right/wrong, all-or-nothing thinking, and focus on the things that make us feel great in our bodies. By employing a more flexible mindset we can live in moderation and achieve our best health possible.

HEALTH AT EVERY SIZE: SCIENCE TO SUPPORT THE BE BODY POSITIVE MODEL

"Health at Every Size maintains that people can follow a healthy lifestyle, have good metabolic fitness, good overall life quality, and reduce risk of disease, no matter what their size."
—Glenn Gaesser, PhD, author of *Big Fat Lies:*
The Truth About Your Weight and Your Health

Health at Every Size® (HAES) is a health-centered paradigm that is being adopted by a growing number of medical and mental health care professionals for use with their patients and clients. And activists and laypeople have joined forces to shift the current weight-centered paradigm—an approach to health that is causing harm to people of *all* sizes—to one that honors genetic diversity and promotes healthy lifestyles for everyone.

Not only does HAES place importance on how we view weight as it relates to health, it also addresses the social justice issues that accompany weight-based discrimination. HAES practitioners worldwide are working with individuals in medical and mental health settings, conducting education and activism efforts to transform people's views about fat, and fighting for human rights legislation at the policy level. Many professional organizations currently work to advance the principles of HAES, including the Association for Size Diversity and Health and the National Association to Advance Fat Acceptance.

HAES Research Shows Balanced Self-Care Behaviors Trump Dieting in Health Improvement

"A number of studies that go back more than fifty years suggest that weight fluctuation, or weight variation—gaining, losing, gaining, losing, over and over again—increases risk of cardiovascular disease by much more than just having a heavy weight itself. So, whenever you read a study that says 'obesity leads to cardiovascular disease,' we have to ask ourselves, 'Is it the obesity [that is causing disease] or the fact that [people are] trying to become not obese?'"

—Glenn Gaesser, PhD, author of *Big Fat Lies: The Truth About Your Weight and Your Health*

In 2005, Linda Bacon, PhD, and Judith Stern, RD, published their findings from a two-year study conducted at the University of California, Davis, in which they examined the health improvements of a HAES treatment vs. a traditional dieting treatment in a group of women classified as "obese" by BMI standards. The results showed that significant health improvements occurred for the women in the study who were able to recognize and follow internal hunger and satiety cues, exercised moderately on a regular basis, and received support to feel better about their size and shape, *regardless of whether or not they lost weight*.[22]

Dr. Bacon's powerful research study revealed that the overall health of the participants (measured by cholesterol, blood pressure, physical activity, and self-esteem levels) was not only improved, but also maintained by the HAES treatment. While the dieting group may have experienced short-term weight loss and health enhancements, no sustainable improvements were achieved. Not only did all of the dieters' health indicators return to their initial measurements, their self-esteem levels were even lower than they had been at the beginning of the study. The dieting group also had a difficult time staying with the program, shown by the high dropout rate. This finding is noteworthy in that it reflects a similar dropout pattern of people who pay diet programs or join gyms to help them lose weight. When the focus of a program is on weight loss, there is a much greater chance of failure—right from the start.

Addressing Skepticism

After teaching people about Health at Every Size, certain questions often arise: *What about morbid "obesity?" Isn't "obesity" linked to diabetes and heart disease? Aren't we in the middle of an "obesity" crisis in the United States?*

Dr. Bacon's analysis of the "obesity" research indicates that we must be thoughtful about distinguishing between association and causality when linking body size with morbidity. Most studies fail to consider the role of "fitness, activity, nutrient intake, weight cycling or socioeconomic status when considering connections between weight and disease." All of these factors, however, contribute to health risk.[23]

Many so-called weight-related issues can be treated effectively *with little to no weight loss*, and solely through positive shifts in eating and exercise behaviors. Individuals vary in how their weight responds to these changes. For example, type-2 diabetics can normalize their blood glucose by adopting healthy eating and exercise habits, even if they are classified as "obese" and don't lose a pound.[24] If maintaining weight loss through dieting is not possible for the vast majority of the population, prescribing a restrictive diet to a fat person is counterproductive, as it tends to lead to poorer physical and mental health and increased weight over time.[25]

The Body Positive's view is that the United States is experiencing a health crisis, and that the emphasis on "obesity" as the problem mistakenly places the focus on body size instead of improving and maintaining healthy behaviors. We are concerned that too many people of *all* sizes:

• Do not have access to and/or can't afford nutritious foods, especially fruits and vegetables, which tend to be expensive.

• Regularly eat highly processed foods and get little exercise. A poor diet and a sedentary lifestyle cause some—but not all—people to put on weight, and this type of lifestyle is unhealthy for anyone.

• Develop imbalanced self-care behaviors in their pursuit of health and thinness (often because they have been told by someone else to lose weight), putting themselves at risk for life-threatening eating and exercise problems.

We strongly believe that shame and blame do nothing to improve a person's health, a belief that is backed by research on weight stigma.[26] We support people of all sizes by offering them our Competencies. Taking weight out of the health equation is a first step.

If you find yourself having resistance to the information you read about HAES, please try to keep an open mind and remember that current approaches to weight and health in this country have not been successful in making our population thinner or healthier in the long term. The quick fixes promised by weight loss programs, TV shows, pharmaceutical companies, and bariatric surgeons result in keeping people stuck in the nightmare of losing weight and gaining it back—over and over again.

Note that the information about HAES offered in this book is merely an overview of a broad topic. If you want to learn more about the science behind HAES, I strongly recommend reading *Health At Every Size: The Surprising Truth About Your Weight*, by Linda Bacon, PhD. A list of other excellent books and websites that explore a weight-neutral approach to health can be found at *thebodypositive.org*.

LILY STOKELY

BODY POSITIVE LEADER
STUDENT OF NATUROPATHIC MEDICINE, BASTYR UNIVERSITY

Today I held a human heart in my hands. A 102-year-old woman who died of old age donated her body to my naturopathic medical school for study. I held her heart that beat approximately 72 times per minute, 103,680 times a day for 102 years. You know what surrounded her heart and fed it so generously for each and every beat? FAT! The heart's preferred fuel is fat! The layer of fat not only cushioned her heart, but fed it as well.

I was speechless as I stood there with the beautiful, pink organ in my hands. Tears welled up in my eyes and I was overtaken with complete and utter appreciation for the miracle of our bodies. I couldn't help but think of all the times I had hated my own fat, wanting it gone. After years of work to overcome body hatred, I now love my body—fat and all. Today, looking at that heart so perfectly created, my appreciation for fat was taken to a completely new level of awe and gratitude.

As I examined the rest of the body, I continued to find special design miracles and their uses for fat: cushioning tendons and ligaments, a protective layer beneath the skin, in the blood stream carrying vital nutrients, on our bellies shielding the organs that give us our life force, on our faces to make our distinct features. Fat is an essential element of our bodies that we can't live without.

I came home tonight and looked in the mirror: I saw my round, beautiful belly, my healthy cheeks and glowing face, my unique smile, my strong, cushioned thighs, and my happily beating heart. I told my fat I loved it from the deepest place of honesty I have ever experienced towards my own body. I want to live to 102 or beyond. I want to be healthy, happy, and have a heart that beats with love and vigor until the very last beat possible.

WHAT *IS* A HEALTHY WEIGHT?

"...health isn't delivered by a medical care system. It doesn't come in neat little packets or pills. It comes from living well—inside ourselves, with others, with work."
—Robert Ornstein, PhD, David Sobel, MD, *Healthy Pleasures*

If BMI is not a good indicator of healthy weight, what is?

At The Body Positive, we believe that healthy weight is achieved by creating a balanced relationship with food, exercise, and rest. This means that *most of the time* we eat when we're hungry, stop when we're full, and eat a wide variety of foods. We stay physically active on a regular basis (even at a moderate level), and rest when we're tired or ill. When we care for our bodies in this way, our weight will stabilize in a range that has been determined by our DNA—our heredity. This is what is known as "setpoint" or "natural" weight.

embody

Exercise physiologist Glenn Gaesser, PhD, describes natural weight in his book, *Big Fat Lies*, as follows:

"Each of us has a 'natural' weight, which we will not find on any height-weight chart. ... Those who are naturally meant to be heavier than culturally or medically imposed standards are healthier when they are heavier; those who are naturally meant to be thinner than those standards are better off thinner; and those whom nature intended to be about average weight are better off at about average weight."[27]

We can attempt to drive our weight below its healthy, genetically-determined, set-point range through restrictive dieting and/or compulsive exercising. However, to maintain that lower weight requires an endless battle and may result in disordered, sometimes fatal, eating or exercise behaviors. We can also drive our weight above its set-point by consistently overeating and/or under-exercising. These are both circumstances that may require help from a health professional to bring us to a place of balance.

When you develop an intuitive relationship with food and exercise, you may lose or gain weight to get back to your easily maintainable range. In the process, it is vital to shift your focus from the number on a scale to the task of caring for your body. With attuned listening to your physical needs for a variety of foods, movement, and rest, numerical measurements are no longer a concern. You maintain a steady size, which will shift slightly depending on factors such as the seasons, menstrual cycles, and travel, illness, or stressful events that may cause you to get away from your regular self-care routines. For the most part, however, you will remain within your individualized set-point range.

Restrictive diets and the weight gain that follows wreak havoc on metabolism and natural weight. Dr. Gaesser explains the "failure" of restrictive dieting and the body's desire for stability:

> "'Failure,' of course, is a purely societal label. For the human body, the post-diet weight gain constitutes a success—success at defending what we call a 'set-point' weight. ... Dieting, then, is an attempt to defy the set-point. Viewed in this manner, dieting is a thoroughly unnatural behavior. When a person's weight falls well below the set-point, the body makes certain adjustments to thwart further assaults on its preferred weight. Ultimately, as the dismal data on dieting failures make clear, the body's set-point is the winner in that battle." [28]

It is important to remember that living in balance means we sometimes get out of balance, and that's okay. With forgiveness and careful listening, we are able to return without extreme effort. If, for the most part, we care for ourselves gladly, our bodies will stay in their set-point range for long periods of time. This range changes over time for both women and men, however, as we experience hormone and other physical shifts during different developmental phases of our lives. These adjustments happen naturally and are not reason for concern, unless they are extreme in either direction.

Take a moment to consider any obstacles that may be keeping you from living in your natural weight range. How can you begin to remove them, embrace the size and shape handed down to you by your ancestors and live more healthfully and joyfully in your body? If you discover obstacles that feel overwhelming to tackle, please seek help from a weight-neutral therapist or health practitioner. The goal is to do your best to love and care for your body, while also taking into account the complexity of your human life.

ELIZABETH

LOVE AND ACCEPTANCE

Self-care is the aspect of our health we can control. I am especially interested in what motivates improved self-care, and that is self-love. Self-hatred and shame do not motivate anyone to take good care of themselves.

However, even people who become incredibly self-loving and attuned to their self-care get sick. No one is always going to be perfectly healthy. As a therapist, I work hard not to judge my clients for their suffering or illnesses. I'm especially careful not to contribute to the double-binding message given to them by society: if they are "faultless" in their self-care, they will become (and stay) healthy. Nothing about this message is true. Even if we take excellent care of ourselves, we might experience illness, accidents, or injuries. Regardless, we will age and eventually die.

A multitude of factors in life affect our bodies, so it's important to have a grateful, accepting, and forgiving relationship with them. I tell my clients to relate to their bodies in the same way they relate to friends. We don't expect our friends to be perfect or perfectly healthy at all times. We don't punish them when their bodies get injured. We see beauty in their idiosyncratic ways, and we love them as they are. It is the same with ourselves; the goal is to develop respect and love for our own bodies, care for them as best we can, and see their beauty—because we love them.

A REASON FOR CELEBRATION

"I really celebrate the person I am. I celebrate others. I look beyond the physical and really get to know people. My relationships with my family, friends, and co-workers—and with myself—have just blossomed because now I no longer see who I am based on numbers on a scale."

—Lisa T., The Body Positive advisory board member

Becoming your own expert provides you with wise and practical information for living in the body you inherited from your ancestors. While genes mainly determine whether you are big, small, or somewhere in-between, it is your lifestyle—how you care for your body in terms of food, movement, rest, and stress reduction—that is the primary determinant of physical wellbeing.

By continually asking the questions *What do I want?* and *How do I feel?* you hone your ability to know what you require to live with the most radiant health possible—in body, mind, and spirit—for your unique life. So, instead of stepping on a scale for information, pay closer attention to your attitudes and how you take care of yourself. Make positive adjustments when necessary, and trust that your body will be what it is meant to be—no struggle necessary. And remember, your body allows you to be here on Earth, which is an excellent reason to celebrate it, care for it well, and give it love as often as you possibly can.

BODY POSITIVE PRACTICES

Explore Your Body Story

The process of becoming the expert of your own body begins by writing what we call your "body story." This practice let's you consciously examine the messages, both external and internal, that affect your current-day relationship with your body. These can range from something specific, such as a single comment that caused you to feel shame about your body, to something broad, such as the pressure you may have felt from the media's impossible beauty standards, or a childhood centered on someone's insistence that you lose or gain weight.

Your story may also include positive communications about self-acceptance—maybe you had a sibling who taught you the value of being independent, or a parent who honored your creativity. Perhaps a trusted person outside of your family told you they loved you unconditionally, just as you were. You'll discover how you may have internalized messages from the outside world, and how these have turned into a critical or supportive voice of your own. The influences you uncover, whether buried deep or on the surface of consciousness, exert a powerful force on how you exist in your body today.

INSTRUCTIONS

You'll begin by drawing your story as a flower, the purpose being that it offers a representation of another living and growing entity. Some people prefer to draw a tree instead—do whatever feels best to you. Remember, this practice is for you only—*you don't have to show it to others unless you want to*—so let go of any critical voice you may have about "not being an artist." Your drawing can be as simple or complex as you'd like; the purpose is to get you thinking about your body story and provide you with useful insights. Make it fun and creative by having lots of crayons, colored pencils, and/or pens on hand.

Roots: Begin by drawing the roots of your flower. Add in (or think about) the primary messages (both positive and negative) you were given about your body from family, friends, your community, TV, magazines, doctors, church, culture, etc., when you were young.

- What were you told about eating and exercise?
- What messages did you get about the size and/or shape of your body?
- Where did you learn what was "acceptable" and "unacceptable" regarding your body?

Stem: Now, draw the stem of your flower. This is where you will explore your current relationship with your body.

- What messages do you get from the outside world, including people close to you?
- How do you speak to yourself about your body?
- What do you believe about health, weight, eating, and exercise?
- How do your beliefs influence your self-care practices and your self-talk?

Flower: End by drawing the petals of your flower to show where you would like to be in your relationship with your body.

- What would a peaceful relationship look like?
- How do you want to feel about your body?
- How could this relationship blossom?
- How would having a peaceful relationship with your body create freedom to be more present and engaged in other areas of your life?

When you're finished with your drawing, take time to sit with it to see if anything else needs to be added. One way to deepen your experience with this practice is to share it with a trusted person. Ask this person to listen to your story without commenting; their purpose is to be your witness. Doing this practice from time to time is an excellent way to observe change and growth. If inspired to do so, you can further develop this practice by writing an expanded body story or a poem, creating a painting or collage, etc.

INSTRUCTIONS FOR GROUP PRACTICE

If you are in a reading group or other type of community setting, you can do this practice together. Designate one person as timekeeper.

a. **Draw your flower:** As said in the preceding individual practice instructions, take ten to fifteen minutes to draw your flower.

b. **Share Your Story:** Each pair up with another person and share your story. You and your partner each take five minutes to explain your drawing. You can share a particular part of your story that has the most meaning to you in the moment, or give an overview of your whole process. As a listener, do not comment, but pay attention to the parts of the story that resonate with your story, and to the things that are new to you.

c. **Introduce Your Partner:** When you come back together as a group, you introduce your partner by giving their name and one specific part of their story that stood out for you. Before doing this, however, tell your partner which part of the story you want to share, and get permission to do so.

d. **Group Discussion:** Once you've gone around the circle and everyone has been introduced, take time to discuss what it felt like to be both a storyteller and a listener. Then, explore the ways in which you have all added to the collective body story of our culture.

A benefit of doing this practice as a group is that you become aware that everyone has a history with their body that informs how they live their lives and interact with others. This knowledge helps to reduce competition and comparison, because we can remember that everyone has both struggles and triumphs in their relationship with their body—we are not alone.

Listening to the Wisdom of Your Body

Learning to sense our health from the inside can be extremely challenging because we are trained to define health by external measures, such as what we weigh, our BMI, and how many servings of vegetables or how much exercise we've had in a particular day. But physical wellbeing is too complex and individualized to be measured this way. Behaviors and food choices that are widely regarded as "healthy" may not be right for your particular body. The only way to know what is truly right for you is to learn through trial and error. One way to get in touch with your state of health is to do a simple body scan. Try this awareness/writing meditation to explore what your body feels like from the inside out.

INSTRUCTIONS

Sit or lie down in a comfortable position. Close your eyes or let them soften, paying particular attention to your breath. Let your awareness float to all parts of your body as you concentrate on internal sensations rather than appearances, numbers, or any "shoulds" you hold in your mind about what it means to be healthy. Notice any judgments that surface, but try to just observe them without giving them too much attention. Ask yourself:

• How do I experience my breath in this moment? Does it feel relaxed or tight? Am I able to breathe deeply into my abdomen and fill my lungs all the way up?

- How do my muscles feel? Do they feel loose? Tight? Sore? Flaccid? Am I holding unnecessary tension in certain muscles? How do the muscles in various parts of my body feel similar or different from one another?

- What do my bones, and the ligaments and tendons that hold them together, feel like right now?

- What sensations are present in my skin? Are these different in different parts of my body? Do I experience my skin as a single organ?

- How does each internal organ that is housed in my abdomen feel? Can I sense how my intestines are functioning in this moment? My stomach? Other organs?

- What does my heartbeat feel like right now? Is it calm? Racing? Beating irregularly? How does my breathing affect the way my heart beats?

- How much am I in touch with my senses? What is my vision like right now? Is my hearing clear or blocked? Is there any sort of taste or texture quality in my mouth? What is happening inside my nose? Is there any scent? Congestion? What is my experience when I rub my hands together and touch my skin? What is the temperature and texture of my skin in various parts of my body?

- What state of mind am I in? How do I experience myself in relation to my surroundings and the people around me (if I'm not alone)? How do I feel being alone?

- What emotions are surfacing, if any?

- How does it feel to be still? Do I need to get up and move in this moment?

- How does it feel if I move around? What kind of movement am I drawn to?

Continue to explore your body in any way you would like. Notice the differences between when you sit or lie still and get up and move. Take time to write down what it felt like to consciously pay attention to all parts of your body. As you get in touch with your physical sensations, you become more closely in tune with the responses to the choices you make, recognizing which ones make you feel whole and healthy, and which ones lead to feeling unwell. In this way, you learn to use your internal wisdom to sense your health from the inside out.

Exploring the Impact of Sizeism on Self-Care and Health

As a society, we have slowly begun to stop making assumptions about people based on race, sex, socio-economic class, gender identity, and sexual orientation. However, sizeism—the hatred, fear, or judgment of others based on the size of their bodies—still runs rampant and unchecked. This form of prejudice continues to exist even though a person's natural weight, like their height, is mainly a reflection of genetics and does not necessarily indicate anything about their lifestyle, personality, beliefs, or background.

It is critical to explore how sizeist beliefs and attitudes have affected your self-care behaviors, and, ultimately, your health. This practice allows you to examine the ways in which you may have internalized messages about the size and shape of your body and the effect this has had on how you relate to and care for yourself. The goal is to become conscious in the face of these beliefs and work to become free so that you can live peacefully in your natural, set-point weight range.

INSTRUCTIONS

Write down the experiences you've had with sizeism, both directly and indirectly, such as comments aimed at you or people in your life. You can also write down your thoughts on societal systems that promote this form of prejudice. Use the following questions to stimulate your exploration:

- How do *you* define sizeism?

- Have you experienced sizeism personally? Witnessed it happening to others?

- How does sizeism affect people on both ends of the weight spectrum? How does it affect people of all sizes?

- How is sizeism similar to or different from discrimination based on other physical traits, such as ethnicity, gender, disability, or age?

- Have you internalized sizeism in a way that affects your physical self-care? If so, in what ways?

- Have you experienced size privilege? For example, can you walk into most clothing stores and find clothes that fit you? Can you fit in airplane seats easily? Does your doctor not bring up your weight during examinations? If so, what does this feel like? How does it have an impact on your relationship with other people?

- How does our society promote size discrimination?

- What do you think about the current societal conversation about "obesity"? How does (or doesn't) it contribute to sizeism?

- Recognizing the problems sizism may have caused in your life and in the lives of people you love, can you commit to a weight-neutral approach to your health and self-care? What would this mean to you? How, if at all, would your self-care behaviors be modified?

Practice Intuitive Self-Care

· ·

GOALS

• Learn to listen to—and follow—your body's wisdom.

• Acquire tools and resources to help you eat, exercise, and live intuitively.

BENEFIT

Trust your innate wisdom to guide daily eating, exercise, and life choices.

· ·

"I had become almost robotic in my checklist of life and it was all about losing weight and maintaining weight loss (weigh myself, report my weight, write down what I ate, count the points, write down how much I exercised, attend meetings). The emptiness of it all really hit me hard this weekend at the Body Positive workshop. I'm not going to waste another minute of my life/time worrying about it. I'm going to trust myself and the inner wisdom of my body, and truly listen to it to guide my eating and exercise habits."

—Cinci S., Body Positive workshop participant

Intuitive (*adjective*):

1. having the ability to know or understand things without any proof or evidence; readily learned or understood (*Merriam-Webster.com*)
2. based on what one feels to be true (*Oxford American*)
3. prompted by a natural tendency (*Dictionary.com*)

Practice Intuitive Self-Care, the second Competency of the Be Body Positive Model, offers a way of relating to food, exercise, and rest—and life in general—that encourages you to learn what is right for your unique experience and to find more pleasure in the pursuit of health. As you'll discover, living intuitively heightens all of your physical senses and puts you in touch with the innate wisdom with which you were born—the best guide there is for making all sorts of decisions.

It's also about learning from trial and error and being kind to yourself when you make "mistakes." You come to honor the life circumstances that make it difficult at times to take care of yourself the way you would like, and simply do the best you can in the moment. How little we would expand our knowledge if we never had to come up against situations that offer opportunities to learn from discomfort. As my mom reminds me when I'm struggling with something, "Remember, Connie, we never learn by doing things right. We *have* to make mistakes in order to grow!"

Doing your best to honor your physical needs isn't always going to look the same. For example, if you have a job, buying food is a different experience than if you are unemployed or are living on a tight budget for other reasons. If you have a difficult relationship with food, doing your best might mean allowing yourself to savor one food each day that you usually feel guilty about eating. Getting exercise can be daunting if you live in an environment where the winter weather is harsh or in a neighborhood where it's not safe to walk alone. Practicing intuitive self-care lets you respond to your body's physical needs and wants *while also honoring your current life circumstances.*

One obstacle that prevents people from trusting their intuition is the thought of being responsible for figuring out what their bodies need. In many ways, this feels harder than having an external "expert" voice tell them what to eat and how to move. But playing with the word "responsibility" makes it much less intimidating: *response ability* simply becomes the ability to respond to the stimuli present. In this case it is *the ability to respond* to sensations of hunger or fullness and the need for movement or rest.

Adding "willingness" to the mix—*ready, eager, or prepared to do something*—positively transforms your relationships with food and exercise even more drastically. When you are willing to adopt this new, intuitive approach to taking care of yourself, then decisions about what, when, and how much to eat, how to move, and when to rest become much easier. You become willing to trust your ability to know what feels good for your unique body, and this infuses your journey with enthusiasm and joy. With more and more research showing a link between happiness and improved physical health, getting enjoyment from self-care creates a win-win situation.[1]

ISA DEL SIGNORE DRESSER

BODY POSITIVE LEADER

My knowledge of intuitive eating began when Connie Sobczak did a training at my high school for students who were starting a group on body image. It was a relief to have someone tell us not to stress so much about "good" food and "bad" food, but instead to give our bodies what they asked for, and to be sensitive about listening to internal cues.

I have no doubt that my ability to live intuitively changed my college experience. I cannot tell you how many times I heard others around me talking anxiously about dieting, exercising, trying to lose weight, and feeling guilty about the foods they just ate. I watched these poisonous thoughts hinder people's self-confidence and take over their lives. Having the internal sense that I could trust my body, instead of what was going on around me, gave me a protective shield. I knew how to quickly change the subject or put in my two cents to say that I didn't think diets worked, etc.

Even when I fell into the cycle of criticizing my body, my practice of intuitive self-care allowed me to quickly brush away the criticism before it cut me deeply. When I heard others begin their rants and bash their bodies, I immediately tuned out their words and tried to physically get out of the situation.

Honestly, not by strict intentions, I have found that I distance myself from those who obsess over food and weight. It is truly harmful to be around this obsession because it spreads like an epidemic.

My journey from having bulimia to creating an intuitive relationship with food was unconventional in that I didn't receive therapy until I'd stopped my binge/purge behaviors. In 1981, there was little public awareness about eating disorders, and not much support for recovery. Learning how to eat and exercise in balance was up to me. I had been listening to weight loss "experts" and dieting friends for nine long years, which had only left me with increased obsession with my body size and the depletion of all things life-affirming. I had no idea what self-care meant, let alone good self-care. All I knew was that I wanted my relationship with my body and food to change.

Once I'd committed to healing, I did receive support from a Los Angeles-based therapist named Dee Downs who sent me a life-saving, isolation-breaking, manila envelope filled with factual information about eating disorders and, most important, one beautifully inspiring story of recovery by Lindsey Hall. Each day I woke up and renewed my vow to become free from my obsession with food and thinness. With my fierce desire to heal and the support of new friends, I moved fairly quickly to a place where my bulimic behaviors ended. The learning process of what it meant to have a peaceful relationship with food, however, was just beginning. At the time, I knew of no resources to teach me how to become an intuitive eater. I was on my own.

At this point, I started therapy with Kim Chernin, author of *The Obsession: Reflections on the Tyranny of Slenderness*, who offered me a feminist perspective on women's struggles with food and the quest for thinness. I became angry at the societal messages that aggressively promoted a single standard of beauty—a standard that had caused me to spend most of my life seeing ugliness in myself and believing my body wasn't good enough the way it was. I also grieved the loss of my teenage years, when freedom and self-love were stripped from me, because I believed what I was told: that thinness was the answer to every problem in my life.

I was ready and willing to take responsibility for what I had done to my body. I chose to rebel against all societal and personal influences that had kept me in a state of suffering. It was time to become my own authority, to learn for myself what was right for me in regard to eating and exercise. Thus began my practice of listening to—and following—my body's wisdom.

My intuitive living practice was difficult at first. Giving up dieting "rules" was scary. Staying with healing required that I leap off a cliff into the unknown, with faith and trust as my only companions. I struggled with quieting the voices in my brain that were screaming for attention, especially the "should" voices from my past that were exceptionally loud. What kept me moving forward was the knowledge that I never again wanted to inhabit the prison I'd built for myself with body hatred. My old ways had nearly killed me. I was determined to create a relationship with food and exercise that brought pleasure instead of pain.

The biggest challenge was learning to sit with discomfort and fear, and to acknowledge, but not follow, the voices in my head that wanted to numb my feelings. This was not easy. In the past, I had turned to food or obsessive exercise every time I had a difficult feeling. My work was to understand that my fears did not go away by swallowing them or trying to literally run away from them. But, facing my worries wasn't as bad as I'd always thought—they seemed to lessen in intensity when I was willing to look at them head-on. Solutions to my concerns presented themselves when I was able to sit through this process.

So, I learned to listen. And by "listening" I mean observing, without judgment, my inner world and the world around me. Instrumental to this practice was developing a set of tools to help me move through the moments when it felt like I wanted to crawl out of my skin to escape myself. One tool I utilized regularly was to get out of my apartment and walk slowly through my neighborhood, paying close attention to the flowers, animals, and people I encountered. Their life force filled me with hope and optimism. I also practiced breathing deeply and paying attention to the sensations in my body when anxiety and stress felt like they were taking over. By sitting still in an observant state of mind, I learned that the tension would eventually pass, and it didn't take as long as I expected.

When I couldn't handle the stress of the moment and was in danger of going back to food or compulsive exercise to cope, I reached out to people who believed in me and inspired my bravery. Much of the courage I needed to follow my new wisdom came from the friends I made at the time.

Slowly but surely, I was able to discern my true voices of hunger and fullness. By taking time to listen, I could hear my body's requests for certain types of foods, as well as for other needs that weren't related to food at all. I also heard its desperate request to stop running compulsively and find balance in my exercise habits.

Listening wasn't enough, though. Trusting the information and acting upon it were next. Looking back, I can see I approached this challenge in the same way I climb a mountain. To get to the top I merely needed to take the first step, put one foot in front of the other, and watch where my feet were going in order to move around the obstacles in my path. I needed only to look up from time to time to determine my direction. A cliché, perhaps, but it really is all we can do. In life, we are frequently beginners. It is much easier to take big risks when we honor the unknown and accept that there is always a beginning, refrain from judging ourselves for what we do not know, and reach out for help if we become lost or afraid.

My internal compass led me to the top of the mountain, to a place of true freedom from my eating disorder and body hatred. I can say without doubt that it was worth every ounce of effort it took to get there.

ELIZABETH

FREEDOM FROM THE "SHOULDS"

An added benefit of learning to practice intuitive eating and exercise is that it leads to using your intuition in all aspects of your life. When we trust what we know about the more basic and primitive things, such as knowing when we're hungry and what our bodies crave, we start listening to ourselves on a more subtle level. Our intuitive wisdom becomes available to help us know the deep truth about who we are, what our purpose is, what's right for our lives, and how we feel in relationships. It is a knowing that provides a guidance system to help us live more peacefully, without a lot of ambivalence and confusion.

Instead of being preoccupied with what everybody thinks we *should* do (which is a very troublesome way to figure out what's right for us), we remain attuned to what *we* know is right for us: we become acquainted with our own truth. No matter how difficult our path may be when we follow our truth, we're not tortured by ambivalence. For example, we may realize we want to pursue a career that is very challenging. If we know in our hearts it is right for us, we have the strength to keep moving towards that goal, no matter what anyone else says about our choice.

Teaching people to listen to their inner wisdom fosters purposeful direction. Those who choose to follow their intuitive knowing go forward with the trust and confidence they need to make positive changes in their own lives and in the world. Even though Connie and I originally started The Body Positive to help teens improve their self-care and heal from eating problems, a much greater gift came about. We saw that when people of all ages became free from their preoccupation with food and perfecting their bodies, they tapped into a huge inner resource that allowed them to share their gifts with others.

INTUITIVE EATING

"When I first started working with The Body Positive, I didn't know if it was possible for me to have a peaceful relationship with food, but I kept listening to everybody else who said it was possible, and that's what I held on to."

—Asiyah A., Body Positive leader

We come into the world knowing how to eat intuitively. There are, of course, rare exceptions such as Prader Willi Syndrome, a genetic condition that causes a person to experience a chronic feeling of hunger, and, thus, to eat beyond physical fullness.[2] Most people, however, are born knowing when they are hungry and how much food leads to satiation. Babies cry when hungry and don't stop until fed. When they are physically full, they will spit out any extra spoonful of food you urge them to take. Elizabeth tells a funny story about trying to overfeed her daughter, Uma, when she was a toddler. As the spoon was coming towards her mouth, Uma looked at Elizabeth and—in true Body Positive form—said, "But Mama, I'm satisfied!"

The problem is that along the way, for a variety of reasons, most of us *unlearn* intuitive eating. The idea that we can trust our bodies to guide us in making positive food choices is totally foreign. Trusting our innate wisdom—especially in making decisions about how to eat—runs counter to what most people (both health professionals and lay people alike) accept as truth.

87

However, the evidence continues to grow in support of intuitive eating as a healthier and more sustainable way to relate to food than restriction and rules.[3]

Intuitive eating is different for every person. I know many intuitive eaters, and we all make different food choices. Some of us are omnivores and others are vegetarians or vegans. Many prefer to eat three meals a day, while a number feel better when they eat smaller meals throughout the day. Some avoid certain foods for various reasons (e.g., allergies, religious customs, athletic practices, illnesses, etc.); others eat all foods. Notably, we are all food experts, *but for our own bodies only.*

The Nuts and Bolts of Intuitive Eating

Elizabeth and I are frequently asked questions about intuitive eating. Below are the ones we hear most often. Answers are based on the research that supports this approach as a healthful practice, and on the experiences of a multitude of individuals who have successfully become intuitive eaters through their work with The Body Positive.

What is intuitive eating? Intuitive eating is the practice of letting your body guide you in choosing what, when, and how much to eat. Eating intuitively means sensing internal signals to figure out what you need, and trusting yourself to make decisions that are both nourishing and satisfying. Rather than relying on external messages to tell you what foods are "good" or "bad," you take time to ask yourself what your body wants in the moment, and do your best to give it what it asks for, no matter how your choices are labeled by others.

When eating intuitively, you slow down and experiment with food. Appreciating its beauty becomes important; smell, color, texture, and taste all enhance the experience of your meal. You pay attention to how you feel after consuming different foods and in different amounts. Through this process you connect with your body in a balanced, healthful, and trusting manner. Eating becomes a practice that has moderation and variety as its core principles, not deprivation.

How will I know when I'm hungry or full? Each person has a unique experience of hunger and fullness. Intuitive eating means listening to your own body's cues, not to someone else's rules or suggestions about when, what, or how much you *should* or *shouldn't* be eating. For some, hunger feels like a grumbling stomach. For others, it presents as a headache, weak shaky legs, dizziness, fatigue, or irritability. Fullness can feel like a heaviness in the stomach, but is also apparent when the food you eat starts to lose its flavor and appeal. If you have a hard time recognizing these signs, it may be that you've learned to suppress your body's signals, and eating on a regular schedule (every three to four hours) will be helpful for awhile. If you continue to struggle with over- and/or under-eating, please seek help from a weight-neutral health professional who can assist you in rediscovering your body's internal cues for hunger and satiety.

What if I eat too much, don't eat enough, or eat the wrong thing? Intuitive eating is a continual learning experience, a lifelong process of trial and error. *It is not a diet.* If you eat more—or less—than feels satisfactory, or if you eat food that causes you discomfort, be kind to yourself. Releasing any guilt you feel for eating beyond fullness, not eating enough to nourish your body, or eating the "wrong" food will give you valuable knowledge that can be applied to future eating experiences. You use these learning times to stay more closely attuned to what your body truly needs. By knowing how you want to feel when you are done eating, and by remembering the experiences of eating different foods in varying amounts, you develop the ability to make balanced food choices more easily. Beating yourself up for making a "mistake" doesn't allow for learning, which means it is easier to repeat uncomfortable events in the future. If you sit with your discomfort and forgive yourself for your perceived error, you have a better chance of remembering the bodily sensations or emotions you don't want to repeat.

Over time, you'll discover which foods tend to make you feel good and which ones don't. You'll learn how much food to eat to reach a state of wellbeing—a state that may not always be the same. Experimenting is an important part of the process. Remember that sometimes you'll choose to eat foods that may not make you feel especially great, but you still might want to eat them to enjoy the flavor. For example, spicy food may give you indigestion, but you choose to eat it from time to time because it gives pleasure to your taste buds. Remember, food does not have moral value, and hunger is not a virtue. Your goal with intuitive eating is to have as many nourishing and satisfying experiences as possible.

Won't I eat "junk food" all the time if I don't restrict myself?
When you are in the habit of restricting what you eat, allowing yourself the freedom to choose any food you want can be scary. In the beginning of your intuitive eating practice, your body (or mind) may be drawn to the foods you have been denying yourself. You may find that you eat more of these foods than you think you "should." If you are listening closely to what your body is asking for, though, you'll find that your craving for these formerly forbidden foods will lessen just by allowing yourself to have them. Over time, you will restore trust in your ability to make decisions about what and how much to eat. You'll learn what foods and in what amounts feel best—on your tongue, in

your stomach, and throughout your whole body. You'll be able to balance the amount you eat of all foods, subsequently removing the need to binge or restrict.

It is important to show yourself that you can have the foods you want. As you repeatedly practice eating behaviors that are relevant to your survival, your brain structure will change, cravings for "junk" food will lessen, and your desire for more nutritious, wholesome foods will grow. Eventually, you will lose interest in eating when you are not hungry and you'll no longer be obsessively drawn to "forbidden" foods. Your ability to nourish your body will improve, and food will no longer hold power over you.

What if I'm hungry for something other than food? We all experience hunger for many things other than food. When you find yourself wanting to eat, take a moment to ask yourself:

- Is it food I'm hungry for, or something else?

- What am I feeling? Boredom? Stress? Anxiety? Grief? Anger? Loneliness? Something else?

- Do I need solitude? Creativity? Community? Movement? Time to breathe deeply? Connection with my spirit? A nap? Contact with another person or pet?

- What obstacles are blocking my ability to meet these needs?

- Will eating food right now satisfy what it is I'm really hungry for?

If it is food you really want, eat it—*and savor every bite!* Remain aware, however, if you are eating to supplant a direct (and perhaps more appropriate) response to needs other than hunger. We all eat for reasons other than physical hunger sometimes—*and that's okay.* It can be wonderful to eat foods that give you comfort, excite your taste buds, or remind you of home. If you can be honest with yourself and make decisions from a place of compassion and kindness—without guilt or shame—you are able to fully explore all of your needs. Letting go of justifying or rationalizing your wants and desires makes it easier to have what you want and desire! Food no longer needs to be a substitute for the things in life you crave. You eat for the simple pleasure of eating, and bravely take steps towards meeting your other needs in suitable ways.

ELIZABETH

SATISFYING YOUR TRUE NEEDS

Sometimes we eat for pleasure; often we eat to improve a bitter chore such as making a difficult phone call or balancing the checkbook. A little treat can make a task we don't want to do more tolerable. Eating can be comforting. We all eat for comfort some of the time, and that's perfectly okay. Problems arise, however, when mindless eating happens on a regular basis, or when we eat to satisfy other intrinsic needs, such as for intimacy, safety, or rest. When we eat when we're not hungry—but to meet emotional needs instead—the food makes us feel physically full, while our hearts are left empty and unsatisfied.

I help my clients who have unbalanced relationships with food discover their self-love in order to know they deserve to have needs—and get them met. Together, we explore that fierce quality of self-love they require to reach out for what it is they're actually hungry for.

When you practice eating in a mindful, satisfying way, you will begin to improve your self-care in other parts of your life as well, such as giving yourself permission to follow your desires, or ask for your needs to be met in relationships. There are many ways to take care of yourself, and eating is just one of them. I hope eating is a pleasurable and beautiful experience for you. If it's not, if you're eating beyond what your body wants and it's hurting you, or not eating enough to sustain you, then it is time to pay attention to and explore your *true* needs. If you can't do this work on your own, please seek out a weight-neutral therapist to help.

What does "Doing Your Best" Mean? Intuitive eating means doing your best to eat in accordance with what your body wants and needs. It is not about being perfect. It isn't always possible to have exactly what you want, when you want it. We are, after all, mere mortals, and situations occur that limit our control. Do your best to keep a variety of foods on hand. Do you need to bring a snack to class or work so you don't get overly hungry? Can you find a less expensive substitute for the food you crave that will satisfy you in a similar way? Is it possible to shop at your local farmers' market using food stamps? Do you need to take steps to make the foods you want more accessible in your community, or for other people not as fortunate as yourself? Be flexible and forgiving when it isn't easy to feed yourself what you want, especially if your budget restricts your choices.

Doing your best means you honor your life circumstances when making decisions about how to nourish your body. Let your senses guide you in having the most pleasurable and healthy experience possible considering the options available to you.

ELIZABETH

EMPOWERING PEOPLE TO OVERCOME DIFFICULT CIRCUMSTANCES

I once had the experience of doing workshops at the same homeless shelter two years in a row. The first time I went, I was worried that teaching the women about the Be Body Positive Competencies wouldn't be relevant to their lives, considering all of the other difficulties they faced. When I returned a year later, I asked the women who had been there previously if what I taught them had been useful.

Many said that what they found the most helpful was the information on intuitive eating: listening to their own bodies, and discovering through trial and error what foods were healthy for them. They said that this focus made them feel less helpless in the face of the agendas and advice that came from the staff of the shelter, especially that which was not always relevant to their experience in *their* bodies.

Another message they appreciated was learning they could make positive choices from the limited foods available to them in the shelter cafeteria. One woman commented that since attending my workshop the previous year she had been concentrating on eating only the cafeteria foods that appealed to her instead of eating those that made her feel bad (and then complaining about it). She said she had started saving her food stamp allotment and on Fridays would go to the farmers' market to pick out the most beautiful melon she could find. She would bring her treasure back to the shelter and savor every moment of eating it. In this way she was able to do what was in her power to improve her health and also to create pleasurable experiences with food, which made her happy.

MARISSA "MS. MISSY" SAUNDERS

BODY POSITIVE WORKSHOP PARTICIPANT
FOUNDER, NIA MINISTRIES AND THE "EXPRESS" YOURSELF
SUPPORT PROGRAM

After many years of living an unbalanced lifestyle, I wanted to become healthy but believed it wouldn't be possible due to my lack of finances. I carried with me the myth that healthy eating meant organic, and organic meant expensive. I believed I couldn't afford to be healthy. By the age of forty, however, and after living for years with various health issues, I decided I wanted to improve my chances of living longer—not just for me, but also for my children and the work I had been called to do. That meant I needed to take action.

I wasn't exactly sure what taking action meant, but I began seeking out solutions to how I could develop a healthier lifestyle. At the time, I was living on a limited budget that included public assistance and food stamps to supplement my income. Early one Saturday morning, I made my way to the local farmers' market and asked various vendors if they accepted food stamps. I was met with smiles and many responses of, "Yes, we do." This revelation allowed me to develop a strategy that consisted of finding interesting recipes, planning my meals, writing out shopping lists, cutting coupons, creating a map for my shopping route so I could buy food at several markets, and cooking more at home.

By shopping at this farmers' market every week, I was able to use and stretch my limited amount of monthly food stamps for fresh fruits and vegetables, bread, meat, and spices. Because I was there so regularly, I developed relationships with the vendors. They offered me extra items for free (even donating to events I coordinated for my work), and allowed me opportunities to sample new foods. I would then go to several other grocery stores to complete my shopping. Each month I had enough food to last, which reduced my level of stress.

It was a lot of work, and at the beginning I wondered if it was worth all the time I spent driving around. But at some point, I began to use my shopping time as my "me time." It was an opportunity to walk around (which meant I was also getting exercise), look at the colors of the food, meet new people, and exchange ideas and recipes. I began to enjoy the time it took to shop every month. I started to look forward to it.

After a year of using this particular strategy, I discovered that I was slowly becoming healthier. My blood pressure that had been high for over ten years was finally normal, and my diabetes was under control. I realized that my strategy to improve my health was working, and that it was definitely worth the effort it took to make positive changes in my relationship with food.

What if I don't like to cook? Cooking is not a pleasurable task for all people. If you don't like to cook, but are the one in your household responsible for making meals or if you live alone, try to make it a creative experience. Ask friends or go on line for easy recipes. Let your eyes take in the numerous colors and shapes in the produce section at the market. See the food as material for an art project. Use your time standing in line at the grocery store to relax your brain, enjoy a good daydream, or people watch. Play your favorite music while you cook. Use chopping time as a way to take out your frustrations of the day (but be careful of your fingers!). Talk on the phone with a favorite person. Make extra food so you can have leftovers in your refrigerator—your dinner tonight can be your lunch tomorrow.

If you are cooking for more people than just yourself, create a sense of community by asking others in your household to join you. If you have children, let them participate in meal preparation from time to time. Give them enough autonomy to make it a pleasurable experience for them—and you! Talk about the foods you're preparing. Taste the foods as you cook. Engaging children in this process is the best (and most fun) way to teach them about nutrition. On days when you really can't stand the thought of cooking, try turning whatever's in your fridge and cupboards into a stir fry or "everything meal." If that doesn't work, get take out or prepared foods—there are lots of nutritious, reasonably priced options these days.

If you know nothing about what foods fuel your body and increase its resistance to disease, gather information about basic nutrition. At the same time, experiment with the information to figure out what works for you and what doesn't.

ANDREA EARLE

CONNIE'S MOM

I have enjoyed cooking since I was a young girl. Even though I grew up during the depression, we always ate well, but we never took our food for granted. When I became an adult and got married, it was to our house that people came for reunions and holidays, and the table would be loaded with good food. Even after my children grew up and left home, I still cooked large meals because my husband Bill had a good appetite. He never once forgot to thank me for the food I prepared. When he died, my life changed in many ways. Cooking and eating alone was a big adjustment.

I would like to share what I've learned in case it helps some-one who has lost a partner or lives alone for other reasons.

It was hard at first to figure out how to shop and eat, but I knew it was important to find a new rhythm and routine. I found it especially hard to cut back on the quantities of the foods I purchased (coming from my depression-era background, I like a well-stocked cupboard!). Breakfast and lunch fell into old pat-terns. But dinner was another thing. This was the time when Bill and I shared our activities of the day, and often played a game of cards afterward. Now I was alone. Dinner had always been a special time for me, and I was determined to keep it so.

Since I like to cook, and choose to feed myself well, I plan ahead for dinner. I live in the country, so take-out isn't an easy option. I buy smaller quantities of my favorite foods because that way they stay fresh. If I cook too much and have leftovers, however, I don't mind eating the same meal twice in a row. I often cook a good amount and freeze some for the days when I'm busy or tired and don't feel like making a meal from scratch. On these nights, thinking about what to eat for dinner feels like a chore, so I pull a homemade soup out of my freezer that will thaw quickly, and make a small salad or toast an English muffin. When I'm feeling this way, I usually give myself some ice cream, too!

I always eat dinner at the table; I make it pretty with candles and flowers. Sometimes I put music on, but not always. I say grace and take a moment to feel gratitude for the food I am for-tunate to have. I admire the plate and the color of each portion; I am aware of each bite. It's much like a Zen meditation. I eat fairly fast because I like my food hot, but when I am through I am aware of being well fed. And I always say thank you to myself for the meal I have prepared. I usually play a game of solitaire before doing my dishes. I don't like rushing off to the kitchen right away, and I want time for my meal to settle.

My dinner routine is a good way to start my evening, which I often spend sitting by the fire with a good book. Though I miss Bill, I'm pleased with the ritual I've created. I have found contentment eating my evening meal alone.

What will happen to my weight if I eat intuitively? Eating in accordance with your body's wisdom may cause you to lose, gain, or not change your weight at all. Regardless, eating intuitively over time will get you to a stable weight range (set-point), and will reduce your chances of the harmful yo-yo cycling that regularly happens to dieters. You'll know when you get to this stable range because your clothes will fit pretty much the same way each day, *which is a great alternative to getting on a scale!* You will probably experience small fluctuations in accordance with your menstrual cycle (if you're female). Illnesses, injuries, stressful life experiences, vacations, long work hours, changing seasons, and travel are other determining factors. It is also a natural and beneficial process to slowly gain weight as you age.[4]

Try not to use intuitive eating as a "good" diet, even if altering your habits causes your body size to change. This will keep you locked into a diet mentality and take your focus away from positive self-care behaviors. Determine success by how your body functions and how it feels from the inside out—not by a number on a scale.

. . .

Creating a new relationship with food was a crucial step in healing from my eating disorder. I had to learn at the most fundamental level how to feed myself. Until that point, I had either binged or starved. And having been a diet junkie since the age of twelve, I knew nothing about what, when, or how much to eat. I started by observing my hunger signals around the standard times for breakfast, lunch, and dinner. I paid particular attention to the consequences of not feeding myself when I was hungry and of eating when I was already full.

A supremely helpful promise I made to myself during those healing days was this: to forgive myself for any action regarding food and eating I considered a "mistake." For the first time in a very long time, I knew I deserved kindness, and realized I needed to commit to giving it to myself. Somewhere in my subconscious mind I understood I was a beginner at learning how to feed myself, so I didn't have expectations of perfection.

There were days when I waited too long to eat and then felt ravenous, which caused me to get out of balance with my food choices and amounts. I was consciously aware that when I got too hungry it didn't matter what or how much I put into my mouth, I just had to eat. When I ate beyond satiety, I took time to breathe deeply into a place of forgiveness. I reminded myself that eating so much didn't mean I had to *keep* eating in the moment because I'd been "bad." Nor did I promise to starve myself the next day, or go on a run to atone. Instead, I saw myself as the mother of a small child learning a new skill, and knew I would never berate my child for eating too much or forgetting to eat.

I developed a decision-making process to help me figure out what to eat when I was hungry. It started with the question, *What do I really and truly want to eat right now?* You'll notice I didn't ask myself *What do I need?* but rather *What do I want?* because *need* at that point in my life was still linked to *should*, and *should* had nearly killed me. This distinction was extremely important in helping me change my relationship with food. The rebel in me has forever balked at the words, "You should," especially when spoken by me—to me!

I gave myself permission to eat foods that had once been on my forbidden list. I practiced eating them without guilt, and slowed down enough to actually taste what was in my mouth. It is important to emphasize here that this process was *a practice*, which means there were times when I felt guilty, scared, anxious, and overwhelmed. As mentioned earlier, in these moments I either reached out for help from people I could trust, or I used relaxation techniques such as walking, meditating, or writing. I trusted that letting myself have whatever I wanted was a step towards healing and kept at it—even when I struggled.

Over time, the obsessive dialogue that swirled through my brain, mostly giving me messages that I was bad and shouldn't be eating whatever I was eating, quieted. Granting myself permission to eat *anything, at any time, in any amount*, removed the power forbidden foods once held over me and ended my bingeing. I no longer experienced "guilty pleasures" because pleasure was positively associated with food. I learned to distrust all messages that use "guilt" in the same sentence as "pleasure"!

How I shopped for food was also important in my process of becoming an intuitive eater. I gave myself extra time to look at food before I purchased it. I tuned in to my body's physical needs by paying attention to the colors and textures to which I was drawn. Was red calling to me? Did I want something crunchy? If yes, then a red pepper was most likely going to be part of my next meal. Did the thought of mashed potatoes make me happy? Did I want a hearty stew? Yes, because it was the middle of winter and my body needed warmth and comfort to get through the dark, cold days. Had the seasons changed? Was my body craving brown rice instead of potatoes? Were the beautiful fruits of summer calling to me? Was I craving protein, veggies, carbohydrates, or something sweet? Did I crave something bitter or spicy? Answering these questions brought a wide variety of foods into my daily meals.

Once, during my early days of healing, I attempted to follow a "cleansing" diet. Four days in I found myself standing alone in my kitchen shouting, "I want cheese!" Realizing the absurdity of the moment, I laughed long and hard—and ate some cheese. It tasted heavenly and I savored every morsel. Obviously, no one had forced me to restrict my food, but I had internalized the cleansing diet's rules about the "right" way to eat healthfully, just as I had when on restrictive diets. But these rules didn't work for me, either. The rebel raised her voice again, and fortunately I listened. If I hadn't, chances are I would have started sneaking behind my own back to eat the cheese!

Standing in my kitchen that day I made a vow to be the ultimate—and compassionate—authority to help me figure out what, when, and how much to eat. It is a vow I have kept for more than thirty years.

Because no food was off limits, I learned over time (and through much trial and error) which ones felt good in my body and which didn't. I did this by paying attention (in a non-obsessive and guilt-free manner) to what I consumed throughout the day and mentally cataloguing how my body felt after eating different foods in different amounts. An internal scanning process of my body and food choices developed, one that eventually became second nature.

Intuitive Eating Tips

1. Allow yourself to eat the foods you are hungry for without the threat of starting a restrictive diet the next day, even if you eat previously forbidden foods. In doing so, you can eat a reasonable, satisfying amount without bingeing, because you know you can have them the next day or even later in the same day. This

state of mind releases the "this-is-my-last-chance-to-eat-what-I-want" feeling that can lead to overeating.

2. Quiet the critical voice that yells at you for eating "bad" food, so you don't have to rebel or numb yourself against it by eating more or less than is physically comfortable.

3. Savor the foods you choose to eat so your taste buds, brain, and all of your senses get as much pleasure from the experience as possible. Fully tasting your food, no matter what it is, allows your body to guide you in how much to eat, because you naturally want to stop when flavor and pleasure diminish. This is a natural signal your body gives you to indicate it's had enough.

4. Keep snacks with you if you are habitually hungry throughout the day. This may mean taking a bit of extra time before you leave the house to prepare food to have with you, but it's worth the effort. It's easy to lose the ability to listen closely to your body's needs when you get too hungry.

Taking the Leap

"The secret of health for both mind and body is not to mourn for the past, worry about the future, or anticipate troubles, but to live in the present moment wisely and earnestly."

—The Buddha

Intuitive eating is a practice that allows us to be fully present in each moment so we can make food choices that are appropriate for our unique bodies and lives. It is a sustainable, positive method for creating a peaceful relationship with food. It honors our intelligence, wisdom, and common sense, frees us from obsession with weight, and provides the opportunity for true physical nourishment. Intuitive eating allows us to do our best in regard to our current life circumstances, honoring that it isn't always easy to have what we want or need.

I know it can be daunting to step away from rules and restrictions about food. I still remember how it felt to let go of believing other people knew better than I what was right for my body. I was scared to trust myself, unsure if my instincts would guide me in a positive direction. Some days it felt as if I were in a tiny rowboat, adrift at sea with no life jacket to save me if the boat tipped over. At the same time, I felt powerful and free. I knew I was in charge of my own life and loved the challenge of trusting my innate wisdom to guide me.

It takes courage to make your own choices about what, when, and how much to eat. Intuitive eating brings you back to the basics: *What do I want?* and *How do I feel?* Through your practice of deep listening, you become intimately aware of your physical hunger and satiety cues and how food feels once it has been eaten. You learn to follow the food you eat all the way through the digestive process to sense what happens as it is absorbed into your body. And you feel the impact of that food on your levels of energy, enthusiasm, and joy.

Experiment to learn what is appropriate for you. Let go of any need to perfect your intuitive eating practice, and enjoy the process of getting to know your body on an intimate level. It is not your appetite or cravings you should fear, but the loss of your connection to the beautiful body that houses your soul.

"It got so pounded into my head that there was no solution for food addiction. I was told, 'If you have an eating disorder you will

have it for the rest of your life, and the only solution is to be completely in control of what you eat.' When I heard Connie's story about recovery and how she now relates to food, I thought, 'There is hope.' Even though I didn't know if I could do it myself, I felt like it was possible, and that was the moment that changed me. I now know it is possible for somebody who had this history to be okay and to come out on the other side and be a beautiful, powerful, brilliant light of hope in the world."

—Asiyah A., Body Positive leader

INTUITIVE EXERCISE

"Activity in and of itself is health promoting, regardless of whether or not people lose weight. It helps lower glucose, it helps lower blood pressure, it increases muscle mass. It's magic."

—Toni Martin, MD

Physical activity is a wonderful thing. It keeps our bodies healthy and strong, and reduces mental stress. Exercise releases brain chemicals that make us feel happy. It can be a social time to connect with friends, or a solo pursuit that gives us time to meditate in motion. The human body is designed for movement; it does not function as well with a sedentary lifestyle. But the demands of the modern world make it difficult to live in rhythm with our physical needs. Many of us have to sit in front of computers all day, or in our cars for long hours as we drive to and from work. Instead of pushing our bodies to the limit every day just to survive, as our ancestors did, we have to think about fitting exercise into our lives in some way, shape, or form.

The primary messages we receive about exercise are that we should do it to burn calories, lose weight, and sculpt our muscles in order to mirror the images presented by the media.

These images have somehow become synonymous with health, though they have more to do with selling magazines, products, and services.

Also, too many people believe the fallacy that only rigorous exercise leads to good health. In their book, *Healthy Pleasures*, Doctors Sobel and Ornstein summarize the results of numerous studies done on the health benefits of moderate exercise. One study found that getting an average of thirty minutes of physical movement per day through activities such as gardening, walking, fishing, dancing, and doing physical chores cut the occurrence of fatal heart attacks in middle-aged men by 40 percent. Increasing the intensity of the exercise and the amount to two hours a day did not make a difference.[5]

This research shows there is a marked difference between the amount of exercise needed to maintain good physical health and the amount necessary to change the shape of your body. I'm not saying there is anything wrong with wanting to sculpt your body or exercise vigorously. It feels good to have strong muscles and to push yourself to see what you can do. But things go awry when an exercise program is based on unrealistic goals focused on weight loss or a particular body shape. Joining a gym in January only to quit several months later because you don't see the results you want does nothing to improve your health.

Ample research proves that staying physically active—not achieving a certain weight—is the key to longevity. Steven Blair, a professor of exercise science, epidemiology, and biostatistics at the University of South Carolina, and former researcher at the Cooper Institute of Aerobics in Dallas, has done extensive research in this area. His findings consistently show that the people who live longer are physically active, *independent of body size*. His decades of research on tens of thousands of individuals consistently produce data confirming that people with large bodies who exercise on a regular basis live longer than thin people who don't. As he told a *New York Times* reporter in 2009, "Obese individuals who are fit have a death rate one half that of normal-weight people who are not fit."[6] Blair, an avid runner, describes himself as "short, fat, and bald" and jokes that running more than 70,000 miles in his lifetime has still left him "short, fat, and bald," but in better physical shape than if he didn't run.[7]

Intuitive exercise honors our need for fun. We may not always feel like exercising, but by listening to our bodies' responses to different types of movement, we learn what inspires us to get up and go. Our motivation is equally as important as having will-power (perhaps even more so) if we wish to stay physically active and increase our chances of living a long, healthy life.

RACHEL MARCUS

BODY POSITIVE VOLUNTEER
PERSONAL TRAINING: FITNESS FOR THE BODY YOU'RE IN!

Before my journey to athleticism, I had a brief and passionate love affair with Jazzercise. This was at a liberal arts college in a small midwestern town. The college students would straggle in, uncoordinated, still in pajamas, and take their places behind the middle-aged women from the town who had been in the class for years. Our hodge-podge group would follow the lead of a short, chubby woman named JazzerPat, who jumped around on a wooden stage and smiled at everyone, even when they were moving in the wrong direction. By the end of the semester, many of the college students had moved to the front of the class.

After a childhood and adolescence of being teased and humiliated by gym teachers, athletic kids, and soccer coaches, this was my first positive exercise experience. I had always assumed sports weren't for me. And, if someone were to tell me fifteen years ago that I'd grow up to be a personal trainer, I would have looked at them as if they had said I would live on Mars. It turns out that Jazzercise class was more useful for my career than anything else I took in college.

Creating a size-positive fitness practice was never in doubt. If I had heard any disparaging body remarks in Jazzercise, or if only thin people had surrounded me, I would have never become the confident fitness enthusiast I am today. I try to bring the playfulness and joy that JazzerPat embodied to the people I work with.

I begin an average day by skipping back and forth across the room with a client, then working with someone with a chronic injury on a balance obstacle course, then counting to twenty for a woman holding a plank position for the first time even though she keeps insisting she could NEVER do that. Later in the day, several people who come to a meeting of my running group are convinced that they need to lose weight before they can "really" run, because this is what the doctor has told them. They leave that same day having run, slowly and steadily, more than they thought was possible, and without any pain in their knees.

Too many of us are convinced that we have obstacles to exercising: that we are too fat, too old, too injured, too uncoordinated. We internalize the gym teacher yelling at us from across the field, or the fitness instructor telling us to "work off those brownies." Simply believing in, honoring, and listening to my clients can go a long way towards shedding these internal obstacles.

The process of becoming more fit is like any other life journey. We make gains by showing up as we are, being willing to make mistakes, laughing, forgiving, and trying again as we develop our muscles.

Learning to Exercise Intuitively

"Fitness should be a healthy pleasure. Popular health advice hypes vigorous aerobic exercise and most often ignores less intense, more enjoyable forms of physical activity. Because of the hype, many people feel discouraged; they can't achieve the ideal prescription of vigorous exercise sessions, and the sleek look of the sinewy models glowing out of magazine covers somehow evades them. So they do nothing."
—Robert Ornstein, PhD, David Sobel, MD, *Healthy Pleasures*

As with learning to eat intuitively, finding exercise that is right for your particular body and life circumstances is a process of trial and error. Our bodies are all made differently and prefer different types of movement. Some people feel better in water, others on land; some feel better doing slow movement, others with vigorous exercise. Each one of our bodies has its own specific requirements for exercise that will support our health.

If you work with a personal trainer or other type of physical fitness "expert," remember to conduct your own experiments to see if the information given to you is appropriate for your body and life. A trainer who emphasizes weight loss may be setting you up for what exercise physiologist Glenn Gaesser, PhD, calls yo-yo fitness (similar to yo-yo dieting) to describe repeatedly starting and stopping exercise programs—and losing whatever gains were made each time. Our bodies stay healthier when we avoid all-or-nothing approaches to both eating and exercise. Physical activity that is sustainable throughout our lifetime is the goal, as well as the key to increasing longevity and reducing risk factors for disease. If you're looking for a trainer, find one who de-emphasizes the importance of weight and BMI, and who works with clients to create exercise habits that are fun and sustainable.

The type of movement that feels best to you may be quite different from that of other people in your life. Your preference may be to exercise alone, or perhaps you enjoy the camaraderie of being with friends or in a class. Time limitations due to a work or school schedule may leave you searching for a half hour here or there to walk or do exercises in your home. Physical limitations or illnesses, and access to a gym might also be factors.

The key is to find activities that you *want* to do—ones that give you pleasure and fit your lifestyle and physical needs—because then you have a greater chance of doing them on a regular basis. I once talked to a woman who said she hated to exercise. I asked her if she liked to dance. She got a big smile on her face and said, "Oh, yes. I love to dance!" She hadn't realized it was a wonderful form of exercise she could do alone or in the company of others.

"When I had an eating disorder, I exercised compulsively in a way that ended up leaving me feeling depleted. Now, since I've started the work towards self-love, I've been able to find joy in my exercise, and it leaves me feeling built-up and stronger."
—Andrea J., Body Positive leader

Becoming an intuitive exerciser took me through a process similar to the one I experienced when I learned how to feed myself again after bulimia. I was an obsessive runner during the years I was trapped in body hatred. My primary purpose for running was to stay thin. I didn't care if I was harming myself by exercising too much; I just wanted to burn calories.

When I made the choice to heal, I had to figure out how to exercise without obsession. I knew I needed to move my body to stay strong and healthy, and to alleviate stress. I also knew I loved to exercise; movement of all types had given me pleasure throughout my life.

At first I backed way off. I stopped running altogether because I wanted to separate myself mentally from the attitude I'd had when it felt like I was literally running to save my life. I discovered that hiking in the hills with my good friend Annie was a pleasurable way to get exercise. We wandered through the hills discussing dreams and goals, not the size or shape of our bodies.

When I allowed myself to return to running on a track, I was no longer able to keep up with the fastest people whose pace I had been able to match before. I created a mantra: "Slower than some, faster than some," I silently chanted every time someone whizzed by, or when I passed another runner. This helped me remember what I loved about running—the feeling of lifting off the ground, getting into a zone where my mind became empty and creative thoughts could emerge, and being outdoors watching the changing weather patterns transform the colors of the San Francisco Bay.

I have learned how to make exercise work for my life. It is something I enjoy, not a chore I must endure based on what other sources say is right for me. My exercise patterns have changed as my life has evolved. I go through phases where I prefer different types of movement, from running on the treadmill and lifting weights at my local YMCA, to hiking in the hills, to doing strengthening and stretching exercises at home, to just doing my errands on foot in my neighborhood.

ELIZABETH

I Love to Move!

I love to exercise. It gives me joy and pleasure so I do it as often as I can. When I use my arms to lift weights, they feel like power-

---

ful tree limbs. Having strong arms makes my household chores easier to do. I like to keep my legs fit by using the elliptical machine at the gym or by hiking up mountains; when my legs are strong I feel better equipped to face the difficulties of life. My strong legs keep me feeling solid on the ground—unbreakable and powerful.

I exercise in order to feel my breath, because when I am breathing deeply I remember what's true. I can *feel* what I know and remember what is important in my life. Breathing helps me get in touch with what I need to learn in the moment; it gives me insights about the truth of my clients' struggles, and reminders of important things to tell my family. Love is one of the central themes that surfaces when I breathe deeply with exercise. I am filled with the desire to tell the people I love how much I love them! I also remember the fun things I want to do in my life, like have adventures.

I also exercise to give my body the treat of physical play. I experience pure bliss doing somersaults in a swimming pool while the rain pours down on a winter's night and the steam rises off the water! It's like a mini trip to Hawaii and I get to have it right here where I live. In these moments I am indulging my body. I believe strongly in the importance of physical play.

Simply put, I love to move. I love the feeling in my body when it is being used, when my muscles are in motion instead of being crunched and tense from sitting in my work chair thinking all the time. Movement brings my center of gravity down from my brain towards my middle, where I feel connected to the earth. Staying strong makes me feel more capable and keeps me from getting injured when I do the things I love to do with my body, like dancing and backpacking. Regular physical movement hasn't changed my size or shape, but it makes me happy and keeps me strong in all areas of my life—and that's what keeps me exercising.

INTUITIVE REST

Being an intuitive exerciser also means knowing when to rest. Listening to your body requires that you honor the times when you are exhausted. In these moments you must discern whether exercise will make you feel better, or if a nap or a day in your favorite chair with a good book would suit you better.

Below is a "recipe" for true rest written by Kate Finney, a Body Positive leader (and therapist), who knows that giving herself permission to rest allows her to exercise regularly and with more pleasure.

KATE FINNEY

Recipe for True Rest

Someone once told me that you never regret a workout. I have to say I completely disagree! I love to be active. I run, hike, go to the gym, and do yoga. Exercise is a huge part of my life. Sometimes, however, I need a break. There are days when my body tells me, "Slow down. Take a load off. You're tired!" By living intuitively and listening to my body, I know that in these moments a workout is not going to make me feel better. Rest will.

Here is my favorite recipe for true rest:

1. Put on a pair of sweatpants and an old t-shirt. Pull hair back. Wash face (no make up!).

2. Make a cup of SleepyTime tea (with honey). Pop some popcorn if there is some in the house (no extra trips to the grocery store—too much work!).

3. Find favorite soft blanket (I keep mine on the couch for just these moments).

4. Get cozy on a comfortable couch or chair.

5. Watch one (or more) of the movies on my "Movies That Always Make Me Smile" list. I highly recommend keeping several of your favorite feel-good movies on hand for true rest days.

6. Finally, and most important, *relax and enjoy—no guilt allowed!*

I leave you with one final thought: because I trust my body, I know that allowing it to rest when necessary does not diminish my desire to exercise on other days. In fact, giving myself permission to rest creates a mindset that makes exercise something I do by choice, something I *want* to do because it feels good, not something I feel forced to do to be good. Listening intuitively to my need for rest as well as movement has allowed me to create exercise habits that I am free to enjoy for the rest of my life.

INTUITIVE LIVING IS A PROCESS

"Listening to my body has given me a much more alive and engaged experience with food and exercise, because I'm operating from how my body feels on the inside as opposed to how I'm supposed to look from an outside perspective."

—Rebecca W., Body Positive leader

Intuitive living is a process. It is not something that you perfect and never struggle with again. It does, however, allow for more flexibility and fun in self-care. It is completely fine to alter the way you eat and exercise, especially if your motivation for doing so is to improve your health and increase your energy level. The basic rule of thumb is to make sure you strive to create *sustainable*, long-term habits. Short-term changes will only create short-term results, and, if they are too extreme, will eventually backfire. Start fresh every day with a commitment to staying closely attuned to your body. You'll be amazed with the results.

BODY POSITIVE PRACTICES

Intuitive Listening

Tuning in to what your body actually needs can be challenging when so many obstacles get in the way of listening to—and following—its wisdom. These may include:

- Eating what you've been told you *should* eat
- Rebelling against "rules" by overeating foods you've been told you *shouldn't* eat
- Getting in the habit of eating meals that are convenient, but not necessarily what your body wants or needs
- Reaching for foods you usually want, even if you're not really in the mood for them in the moment

The goal is to find a sustainable, pleasurable way of giving your body the nourishment it needs to thrive. In the process, you learn the difference between instant gratification (which is perfectly fine from time to time) and knowing what makes your body feel best in the long run. For example, certain foods may give you a good feeling in the moment, but you know that they cause you to feel sluggish or uncomfortable later on. And remember, you most likely *will* get out of balance with your eating habits every so often, even as an intuitive eater. But what you will learn is that getting back into balance isn't all that hard when you remember to listen closely to your body. This practice can help you clear away some of the noise in your head so you can figure out what, when, and how much to eat.

INSTRUCTIONS

The next time you're in the mood for a snack or meal, try this meditation. Sit or lie down in a comfortable position and take several deep breaths. With each breath, pay attention to different parts of your body. If you notice judgments coming up, just observe them and keep breathing. For now, put aside all ideas about the "right" way to eat. While paying attention to each of your five senses, ask yourself:

- What sensations do I feel right now?

- Am I physically hungry? What sensations let me know whether I'm hungry or not?

- If I am hungry, what do I really want to eat right now? Is it something savory, sweet, cold, hot, crunchy, soft?

- Is there a certain combination of foods that will give me the most satisfaction?

- Do I want to eat alone? With other people?

- Is there anything stopping me from having what I want?

- Am I too hungry to be able to get in touch with what my body really needs?

- What sensations are telling me if I'm hungry for food or something else?

- If I'm not hungry for food, what is it that I really need? Movement? Rest? Company? Solitude? Support with an emotional issue?

Once you've explored your current needs, try to give yourself what would be *most satisfying*, whether that is food or something else, getting as close as you possibly can. You may not be able to have exactly what you want in the moment, but take note and think about how you can get these needs met more reliably in your life.

Practice this meditation as often as you can before eating a meal. Over time, as you get better at listening to your body and hearing what it wants, you will do this process on a more unconscious level. If you repeatedly come up against obstacles to eating in a balanced manner, explore the following questions:

- What obstacles are stopping me from listening to my body's wisdom in making decisions about feeding myself?

- How can I overcome these obstacles? Do I need support from a professional?

Remember, learning to eat intuitively is a practice—it doesn't happen overnight. If you've had serious struggles with food, you will want to take this process slowly, honoring any needs to continue following a food plan or other structured approach until you're ready to fully trust yourself to decide what, when, and how much to eat.

Letter to Your Meal

Learning what your body needs for nourishment as well as pleasure means paying attention to how you feel after eating a meal. This is what making food decisions by trial and error is all about.

Ask yourself:

• What worked?

• What didn't?

• What did I learn for next time?

INSTRUCTIONS

After eating your next meal, get out a piece of paper or your journal and write a letter to the food you just ate. Do this in whatever way feels best, but take note of the different aspects of the food (texture, taste, color, temperature, nutrients, amount, etc.) and how your choices worked or didn't work well for you in this particular moment. Some people like to write straightforward letters, while others prefer to write a poem to celebrate their meal. You may find it feels good to add a note of gratitude to the food for giving you nourishment, pleasure, etc., or forgive it for not being what you wanted. Do this practice whenever you feel the need to more consciously pay attention to how you are feeding yourself. It may sound strange to write a letter to your meal, but it's a fun and creative way to experiment with food choices.

Intuitive Exercise: What Do I Know?

Intuitive exercise is about finding movement that feels good to you on many levels. It's not just about burning calories or "getting in shape." This practice offers an exploratory process that can help you get more in touch with your motivation for physical activity.

INSTRUCTIONS

a. **Exploring Messages:** Take some time to explore what you've been told about exercise. Can you recognize any external voices, such as those of a parent, coach, or friend that may have influenced how you choose to move your body or feel about exercise in general? Write down your answers or, instead, just think about what came up, or share the information in conversation with someone you trust.

- What messages did I discover (both helpful and hurtful) that come from other people?
- How do these messages influence my attitudes and behaviors about exercise?
- How do they influence my motivation?

b. **Deepening the Process:** This part of the practice offers a meditation that deepens your connection with your body and your motivation for exercise. Close your eyes and imagine an experience of physical activity that made you feel completely alive. You can ask yourself the questions below to prompt your imagination. If you've never had a positive experience moving your body, use the questions to think about what this *could* be.

- Where was I?
- Was I alone or with others?
- Was I indoors or outside?
- Was I in a city or in nature?
- What was it about the experience that made me feel especially great in my body?

Write down what came up for you, or give yourself time to ruminate on your answers. Use the questions below to continue your exploration.

- What did I discover about my relationship to exercise?
- Is there anything about this relationship that I need to let go of? Any beliefs or behaviors that are more destructive than helpful?

- Are there actions I want to take to bring more pleasurable movement into my life?

I recommend doing this practice as changing life circumstances and/or developmental life stages create new situations that affect how you want or need to keep physically active.

Create Your Own "Recipe for True Rest"

It is vitally important to find ways to deeply rest your body. Doing so not only helps you physically, but also gives your mind a chance to take a break, which leads to better functioning for all that is required of you. Quieting the body and mind gives your heart a chance to speak, a voice that can be overlooked when there is too much activity and noise. Even taking just a few moments to be still will provide ample benefits on all levels—body, mind, and spirit.

If you didn't worry about what other people think, or what your inner critic says to you about why you shouldn't take time to relax, *what would you do to let your body completely rest when the need arises?*

INSTRUCTIONS

Give yourself what you need right now to really let go. Take time to sink down into a relaxing nap, or sit quietly just observing a garden or the sky. Maybe you need soft music or a good book. Think of the times you have rested deeply, what was the situation that allowed this to happen? What would make it possible for you to rest now, in this moment? Think about your own "recipe for rest," and use the same trial and error process you use with eating or exercise to bring those ingredients into your life.

A Sensual Exploration of Food: Group Practice

A fun way to explore intuitive eating is to do it with other people. The following is a practice of simply observing your food choices without judgment, even if you make what you consider "mistakes."

Before you begin this practice, discuss how there are no right or wrong choices, no "bad" or "good" decisions. You will want to agree to suspend judgment about yourself and others, as well as any conversation about the "best" way to eat. Also agree that if anyone starts to talk about calories, weight, diets, etc., others can intervene and bring the focus back to the purpose of the exercise, which is discovering what foods feel right for each person.

INSTRUCTIONS

a. **Bring a Variety of Food:** Have each person in the group bring a different food, or have one person bring an assortment and everyone can pitch in for the cost. You'll want a variety of textures, colors, and flavors. A snack could be a variety of fruits (strawberries, grapes, small oranges), nuts, chocolate, other non-chocolate sweets, and something salty such as pretzels. For a full meal, you'll want to think about having choices from various food groups. Set out the snacks or meal on a table where everyone has easy access.

b. **Choose Your Food:** As you choose what you want to eat, pay close attention to the color, texture, and overall appearance of each food. You can use the following questions to guide your decisions:

- Do I want something crunchy, juicy, colorful, bland, squishy, sweet, hot, cold?

- What does my body want right now?

- What does my mind want?

- Are there certain combinations of these foods that look good together?

- If there are no restrictions, rules, or judgment, what do I really want to have right now based on what is available?

It's okay to nibble a bit as you go to your seat, but save most of the food for when everyone is back together in the group.

c. **Chat and Chew:** Use the guidelines below to heighten your awareness as you eat and as springboards for discussing the experience.

- Study the food on your plate. How does it look?

- Without judgment, think about why you chose the food on your plate. What went into your decision-making process? Do you like your decisions? Did you forget something? Is there a food on your plate that you now don't want to eat? Take time to get it right—remove what you don't want and go back for anything you do.

- Now, look over your plate and choose what you want to eat first. It may be one thing or it may be a combination of foods. Put the food under your nose. Do you like the smell?

- Take a bite. Chew or suck on it slowly. Let the food start to mix with your saliva to give you maximum flavor. How does it taste? How does the texture feel in your mouth? Can you still smell its aroma?

- Now swallow and see how it feels going down. Was it the right choice? If you don't like the flavor or texture of what you chose, pick something else. If it felt right, do you want more of the same or do you now want a different flavor?

- How much do you want? Are you hungry right now? Listen to what your body is telling you. Listen closely!

- Talk about what it feels like to slow down and be consciously aware of the choices that go into each bite.

Group Discussion

You can expand your group discussion with the following questions:

- Why is it so hard to listen to our own bodies' needs for food, movement, and rest and so easy to listen to what other people say about what we "should" do?

- What happens when we label foods "good" and "bad"?

- How do we feel when people talk about being on a diet? Or say they're "bad" when they eat foods labeled "non-nutritious"?

- How do we feel when people talk about their specific eating habits? Especially if they express anxiety?

- How do we feel when we walk into a grocery store? Restaurant?

- Why is a person with an appetite for food and for life threatening to others?

- Why has eating become so complex in our culture?

- Knowing we can't always take so much time to look at and smell our food before we eat it, how can we bring even a bit more conscious awareness to future meals so we'll get closer to making choices that satisfy us—body, mind, and spirit?

This practice can also be incorporated into other kinds of gatherings. If your group shares food, eat together in a conscious manner, and have a short discussion about how everyone is doing with their practice of intuitive eating.

Cultivate Self-Love

....

GOALS

- Develop a practice of self-love.
- Employ compassion, forgiveness, and humor as you leave behind the need for self-criticism.

BENEFIT

Gain confidence and free up energy to make life-affirming choices.

....

"The work of self-love honors the voice of the heart. While we cannot always remove our critical voices or fully insulate ourselves from things beyond our control, we can choose what we take in. Self-love allows me to know I am exactly enough, just as I am. It is the voice I have learned to fine-tune like a radio station so that its kind and compassionate messages make the critical voices fade. Self-love protects my heart, despite the inevitable sorrows of life."

—Jessica Diaz, The Body Positive board member

After years of avoiding the "L word" in public because we were advised that it would turn people off, Elizabeth and I decided to honor what appeared to be a radical aspect of our work—we began speaking directly about love. **Cultivate Self-Love**, the third Competency of the Be Body Positive Model, helps you dig deep inside to find a compassionate, gentle, and forgiving voice to guide and protect you. Embodying this Competency leads to increased confidence and a more positive, peaceful existence, because it diminishes the power of the critical voices that perpetuate insecurity and fear.

In 2007, a producer from Oprah's talk show called because she had heard about The Body Positive and was intrigued by my stories about our young leaders. This prompted me to put together a short video to share their voices directly. At the time, we were having conversations with a publicist who told us not use the expression "self-love." Her opinion was that we needed to tone down our language and talk about "acceptance" in order for people to relate.

In my attempt to follow this advice, I asked the students I was interviewing to refrain from saying *self-love* in describing how The Body Positive had transformed their lives. Despite the various ways I requested that they rephrase their answers, none of the interviewees could do it. This experience confirmed for me that cultivating self-love is an integral component of our message; it *is* possible to go from self-criticism (or even stronger feelings of self-hatred), *beyond* mere acceptance, to a deeply-rooted love for oneself.

Knowing we deserve to have this quality—and making the commitment to reach for it when we struggle—ignites a transformational process that allows a whole host of positive changes to occur. The most profound I've observed are: the development of trust in the body's innate wisdom to guide physical and psychological self-care; improved interpersonal relationships; and the integration of body, mind, and spirit to support more purposeful living.

An added bonus of pursuing self-love is that it will positively transform your self-care behaviors. Eating in a balanced manner and exercising regularly become activities you *want* to do because they enhance the good feelings you experience from being kind to yourself. You may have been taught that being critical of your body is good motivation to improve your self-care habits. It is the old notion that you can "whip yourself into shape." In actuality, the complete opposite is true. With self-love you ask *What is it I really want or need right now?* Over time you are able to answer this question with ease; your response will take a number of forms, depending on what is right for you in the moment.

Loving your body allows you to hear its wisdom; it will tell you exactly what you need to thrive. With self-love, you develop more attuned listening skills. When you don't listen, don't act upon what you've heard, or make what you think of as a "mistake," you use these experiences as opportunities to learn more about what feels right. Instead of letting your critical voice beat you up, you employ kindness so these "mistakes" can be the teaching moments that remind you of how you want to feel the next time you're presented with the same situation. Being mean to yourself only makes it harder to learn the lessons, and chances are you'll have to repeat the difficult experiences until you're able to respond with kindness. This practice ultimately leads to more time spent in situations (in all aspects of your life) that offer pleasure and good health.

KELLE J.

THE BODY POSITIVE BOARD MEMBER

When I first came to The Body Positive, my emotional self was buried beneath hardened layers of suffocating shame and grief. I had been in and out of therapy, recovery programs, and support groups looking for a way out of my self-loathing. Something in me wanted freedom, but each time I began to thaw, the emotional pain became too much to bear, and I made a run for the door. It felt impossible to follow the positive, constructive steps the therapist or program prescribed, reconfirming my deeply-held belief that I was so damaged that there was no possibility of redemption.

The Be Body Positive Model and community were different. When I first heard Connie and Elizabeth talk about self-love, I rejected the notion for myself out-of-hand; I had embodied my shame for so long that I hardly had a self at all, let alone one I could love. I had a core belief that I did not belong in the world, which made me feel unique in my conviction that I was inherently flawed: *Self-love is possible for you, but not for me.*

However, what I also heard at The Body Positive was that there was no possibility of failure here; that the Competencies were not just another set of rules I would surely fail to follow. Instead, I was invited to engage in a process of trial and error where the "errors" were met with gentleness and represented learning opportunities—not evidence of my weak and defective nature. Most important, I didn't have to get self-love "right" to belong in this community. What a gift this is! I am still chipping away at the geological layers of shame and self-loathing that sometimes weigh me down, but have been held with love in The Body Positive community long enough to witness the journey to self-love in others, and think to myself, "That could be me one day."

DEFINING SELF-LOVE

"Practicing self-love means learning how to trust ourselves, to treat ourselves with respect, and to be kind and affectionate towards ourselves."

—Brené Brown, PhD, LMSW, *The Gifts of Imperfection*

Self-love in Body Positive terminology refers to loving our *whole* selves, bodies included. It is a state of mind, which means each and every one of us is allowed access, no matter who we are or what we look like. Self-love is not static, arriving one day and staying for the rest of your life. It is a daily practice—emphasis on the word *practice*—built on a foundation that grows stronger with time and attention. In the same way you must forgive yourself for making "mistakes" as you learn to eat and exercise intuitively, cultivating self-love requires that you absolve yourself when your critical voice arrives for a visit in your brain, even for an extended stay! With practice, you hear the mean voice as it begins to speak, learn to honor its presence, and do the work necessary to become less fearful. As your self-love grows in strength, you will discover an increasing capacity to respond to your critic in a manner that allows you to return to the awareness that you are worthy of love and respect just as you are— especially from yourself.

As self-love becomes a habit, you are less inclined to let your life force be drained away by the dictates of individuals or industries that profit from your attempts to achieve an exclusive standard of physical beauty. Instead of thinking that having a "perfect" body leads directly to self-love, you understand that self-love allows you to see yourself as perfect, "flaws" and all. It moves you beyond a begrudging acceptance of your body, age, or other characteristics, and supports that next big (and often scary) step towards truly loving your whole self—right here, right now. Your perceived "flaws" then become a portrait of your life story—your ancestral inheritance—and an integral part of your beauty.

I've noticed that the word self-love has entered the common lexicon of the mental health field and is no longer a taboo subject. My concern, however, is that its meaning is debased by people who preach the message that if you love yourself enough you are guaranteed to lose weight. A practice of self-love will most likely lead you to more balanced self-care, but it is not a diet.

We do not know what will happen to people's body size when they begin to love and care for themselves. Individuals who have been bingeing regularly or living a sedentary lifestyle may lose weight over time. Those who have been severely restricting or over-exercising may gain. Others will stay exactly the same for a number of reasons, such as a slowed metabolism from yo-yo dieting, or because they are already at their set-point weight.

True self-love offers so much more than weight changes or physical perfection. It expands our view of our whole selves (bodies included), our purpose, and our outlook on life. It provides the opportunity to live fully in the present and to stop waiting for some magical transformation to happen before we pursue our dreams and desires.

Self-love is a quality that has not been role modeled to many of us, and it is certainly not a common topic of conversation. Regardless, we can cultivate it as a daily practice and open ourselves to a new way of experiencing the world.

ANDREA JERGESEN, DO

BODY POSITIVE LEADER

Born in September, I am a Virgo through and through: organized, methodical, exacting, attentive to detail. Amusingly, this set of characteristics produces horoscopes that often sound slightly apologetic, "So Virgo, I know you've been working hard, but this month maybe you should try to let go, relax, let that hair down..." In kind terms, the astrologists of the world are often trying to get me to calm down. And as hard as it is to admit it, they are often right.

In college, I learned the hard way that the same type-A characteristics that allowed me to excel at school were dangerous when applied to other areas of my life—particularly, my body. With a best friend majoring in food justice and agriculture, I became more and more educated about nutrition. As with academics, I applied myself to the new project of learning how to "eat healthfully" with gusto and exactitude. Slowly, what began as a benign experiment in eating more plant foods and being mindful of food labels turned into a compulsive and restrictive eating pattern that caused me to become underweight and unhealthy.

At the end of my undergraduate career, ready to heal, I landed by a stroke of grace on the doorstep of The Body Positive. As I learned about self-love and intuitive eating and exercise, light bulbs lit up in me; I had a soaring sense of excitement and hope, and vowed that I would become a complete expert in self-love by the end of the week. Watch out world, here comes the most perfectly and completely self-loving woman you have ever seen!

Alas...my ballooning energy was gently deflated as the wise women of The Body Positive observed that in my quest for perfect self-love I was resurrecting the pattern of exactitude and control that had led to my eating disorder. Then came the biggest light bulb of all: perfect self-love means being imperfect all the time, and loving yourself anyway! Again and again, being self-critical, self-loathing, self-destructive, and then looking in the mirror and saying, "Whoops! Let's try that again. I love you, you perfectly, beautifully flawed, and fabulous being. We'll get it next time—maybe!"

Learning this lesson gave me an immense sense of relief; I could calm down. I saw myself for who I was, not who I thought I should be. I beheld beauty and intelligence, not flaws and deficits. I was a perfectly imperfect human, just like the rest of the world around me. I was humbled, and instantly connected to humanity in a way I never had been. This, perhaps, has been one of the greatest gifts of all.

Another Virgo trait is a dedication to service, and for me this has played out in my becoming a physician. I am grateful to know that because of my practice of self-love, I may maintain my attention to detail, efficiency, and organization for the benefit of my patients, but I also have the depth of heart to know that as I stumble in my self-love, so will my patients in their pursuit of health. Nonetheless, just as I will keep loving myself, I will keep caring for them. Unconditionally. I can't wait to see what will happen. Watch out world, self-love is more radical than perfection.

RESISTANCE TO SELF-LOVE

"Love yourself first, and everything else falls into line. You really have to love yourself to get anything done in this world."

—Lucille Ball

Talking about self-love may sound cheesy or a little "out there." You may be thinking—as many do—that it is something others can have, but not you. One of the reasons people struggle with this concept is because one who possesses self-love is deemed conceited, narcissistic, and uncaring of others. A case in point is the Merriam-Webster online dictionary definition of the word as "conceit" and "regard for one's own happiness or advantage," which says a lot about why people have a hard time believing it is a worthy pursuit.

My curiosity about the negative definitions of self-love and people's resistance to it led me to a blog written by a psychologist who linked it to narcissism, selfishness, and even ruthlessness. He also (thankfully) mentioned the work of philosopher Jean-Jacques Rousseau, who made a distinction between two types of self-love. *Amore propre* (often listed as a synonym for self-love in thesauruses) has the negative associations many people think of, including hierarchy, comparison, and competition. *Amore de soi*, on the other hand, is something humans are born with and a trait necessary for self-preservation in all animals. Rousseau described *amore de soi* as a quality that leads to more humanity because it is not associated with self-interest, but rather individual wellbeing. It allows humans to be aware of their valuable existence and does not elicit any need for comparison or competition.[1]

Dr. Brené Brown's extensive research on shame, vulnerability, and wholeheartedness (work that has gained considerable attention since her TED talk in 2010) led her to the realization that "a deep sense of love and belonging is an irreducible need of all women, men, and children." After analyzing the stories of thousands of people, she concluded that, "Love is not something we give or get; it is something that we nurture and grow; a connection that can only be cultivated between two people when it exists *within* each one of them—we can only love others as much as we love ourselves." Dr. Brown emphasizes that pursuing self-love must be a priority, and sees it as a revolutionary act, especially living in a society where we are encouraged to put ourselves last.[2]

In the early days of The Body Positive, we became aware that self-love was a revolutionary idea. We saw it as an extremely important quality for all people to possess, and essential to those who are healing from eating problems and body dissatisfaction. Though we continued for a time to water down our language by talking about acceptance, we always came back to the knowledge that people benefited greatly by taking that big—*radical*—step and committing to a practice of self-love.

We offer the message that choosing to love ourselves just as we are is a bold act that goes against the conditioning most of us receive from society, friends, and often our families. It is much easier to fit in when we participate in the self-critical rituals going on around us, but doing so means we must betray our souls. The Body Positive is an alternative community where the pursuit of self-love over self-criticism is the norm. For many, this truly is a radical idea.

Also noteworthy is the field of research that has emerged to study *self-compassion*. Recent studies suggest that the more compassion people have towards themselves, the healthier and more productive they are.[3] This research appears to support the results we have observed when people practice self-love. Kristen Neff, PhD, a self-compassion researcher at the University of Texas at Austin, stated in a 2011 *New York Times* interview that, "Self-compassion is really conducive to motivation...With self-compassion, if you care about yourself, you do what's healthy for you rather than what's harmful to you." Dr. Neff discovered that most people's anxiety about having self-compassion is they fear becoming self-indulgent. Her research disproves this concern: negativity and self-judgment leave us *less* motivated to take action to improve our health and wellbeing.[4]

Elizabeth and I choose to use the word *self-love* because it includes deep feelings of affection along with compassion. Love is the quality that dissolves negativity and self-judgment, freeing us to fully inhabit our bodies and lives, care for ourselves well, and passionately pursue our goals.

Numerous individuals who work with us have said that embodying the Competencies of the Be Body Positive Model caused them to "fall in love" with themselves. As Dr. Brown's research shows, this is not a narcissistic pursuit, but rather an essential way for people to see themselves as whole and worthy beings who deserve to be cared for and treated well. It is what Rousseau described as *amore de soi*.

In *Born to be Good: The Science of a Meaningful Life*, psychology professor Dacher Keltner, PhD, discusses the science that shows "loving relationships (of any kind) lead to less depression and anxiety, greater happiness, more ruddy health, a more robust nervous system, and greater resistance to disease (not to mention it just feels good)."[5] I know from my own experience, and from the stories told to me by scores of others in The Body Positive community, that loving one's self allows people to experience the benefits Dr. Keltner mentions in connection with being in "loving relationships of any kind." Happiness, optimism, and other positive emotions have been shown to contribute to improved health and longevity.[6-7] If self-love leads to more moments of optimism and happiness (people are certainly happier and more hopeful when their loving voices override their unkind critical ones), then it is reasonable to assume that loving one's self offers the same benefits.

Practicing self-love does not in any way mean we ignore our shadow sides. Truly loving ourselves means we honor and respect all of our emotions. When I know my critic will not attack me for feeling angry, sad, hurt, shame, or other difficult feelings, then I am safe to face my experiences head-on. Even if my critic does speak, I know I have the resources to quiet its voice so I can be fully present with whatever I'm feeling. The so-called "negative" emotions give us great opportunities to learn and grow. If we know we possess a foundation of self-love—the kind that promotes self-preservation—then we can take the risk to dive into our suffering to learn what it can teach us.

If you find yourself having resistance to the idea of self-love, I gently remind you to keep an open mind. You may still think it's something you can't have, but that's just fear talking. Chances are, there was a moment early on in life when you didn't have a critical voice. Though that may never be the case again (I think it's nearly impossible to live without any trace of a critical voice, especially in this society), you can learn how to work with your critic to afford it less power. Knowing that self-love is not one more thing to perfect makes it easier to pursue. Since there is no room for failure, there's nothing to lose and everything to gain.

Wholly Mine

No longer addicted to a lifestyle unsustainable
I'll save being a skeleton for when I am dead, please
My essence lost in fake-smiling pictures
A chain-link fence around my mind
"I love you," I said to myself,
But you're hurting me. So I must leave now"
I dropped some love in my empty eyes
Sensation moved in where fear had lived
I finally understood what freedom meant
The deepest connection lies within the soul
Divine again, but more so,
I became
Wholly...
...Mine.

—Sophie Linder, Body Positive volunteer

ELIZABETH

SELF-LOVE IS THE ROOT OF ALL HEALING

Nothing is more important than cultivating self-love. I'll never forget driving home after dancing one morning and getting in touch with the powerful realization that loving myself is the most useful step I can take on my spiritual journey. It became absolutely clear in that moment that the primary work people must do is to reach for self-love no matter what is going on in their lives. What a gift I received after a long day of seeing clients when I recognize that my job is teaching people to love themselves. I have a great job!

The most useful tool I offer clients to help them overcome eating disorders, depression, relationship struggles, or difficulty coping in the world, is to listen to their hearts and reach deeply for the resource of self-love. Forgiveness and mercy allow us to pick ourselves up when we fall, dust ourselves off, and keep moving forward in the face of all of life's difficulties and losses. I help my clients understand that self-love is the answer to all of their struggles:

How will I protect myself in my relationship? Self-love.

How will I know when I am hungry and feed myself what my body needs? Self-love.

How will I learn to stop eating when I am physically full? Self-love.

How will I recognize my needs and get them met? Self-love.

When my clients ask, "But what about the whole conceit thing? Won't self-love make me vain?" I carefully explain that conceit and self-love are not synonymous. Conceit is competitive and cold. Self-love is warm and connected.

When my clients express hatred for themselves and hurt themselves with self-destructive behaviors, I don't try to cure them with my love. I talk to them about being fierce and reaching for their *own* self-love rather than seeking it from others in order to feel validated and seen.

Being kind and loving with yourself is reflected back to you in your relationships. You can confidently be seen by other people because your heart says, "I'm a good person. I'm not perfect, but I am worthy of kindness and respect."

Self-love is the greatest gift you can ever bring to a relationship. Giving your child, partner, friend, parent, or sibling an uncomplicated "seeing them" that comes not from competitiveness or criticism, but from your love and confidence, is a precious gift. It is from this place that you are capable of offering others the opportunity to see themselves through their own loving gaze. Self-love is the root of all healing.

BILL MARZOLLA

NASM CERTIFIED PERSONAL TRAINER

First and foremost, I am a product of The Body Positive. Connie Sobczak—my aunt, lifelong mentor, and one of my best friends— has always been there for me. If it weren't for her and the self-love ideology that is the foundation of The Body Positive, I would not be the emotionally and physically healthy man I am today.

Nor would I be so helpful to my clients as a personal trainer.

In my childhood and adolescence, Connie taught me an important lesson: that regardless of my appearance or fitness level, I deserved to love myself. Love is so important to our existence; so important, in fact, that psychological studies have shown that if an infant were provided with all of the necessities for survival but deprived of love, it would die. Regardless of whether anyone thinks I'm attractive or ugly, fat or skinny, smart or dumb, or any other arbitrary labels that people place on others, I will always be good enough for myself.

Connie once told me, "I have the best job in the world because I basically just get to love people for a living." In my own way, through teaching people to exercise because they love themselves, I am doing the same thing.

THE CRITICAL VOICE

"This is your life, right now, on this changing earth, in this impermanent body, among these excruciatingly ordinary things. This is it. You will not find it anywhere else."
—Sue Monk Kidd, *The Dance of the Dissident Daughter*

If self-love is a trait needed for self-preservation in all animals, why is it so elusive to humans? Why do we have critical, nasty voices inside our heads that lash out at us for not being perfect, for making foolish blunders, for the appearance of our bodies? Why do we not treat ourselves with the same respect and love we give to others?

The critical voice is fear talking. It is the mind's way of attempting to protect us when the world is harsh. As children, many of us were never taught how to resist aggression. We weren't given the tools we needed to hold on to self-love when we were faced with the frightening outside world. Our minds thought people were mean to us because we were flawed. No one told us otherwise, or if they did, we didn't believe them. As adults, we may *still* believe that we will be safe from hostile acts if we can perfect our bodies and lives. When someone gets angry with us or treats us with disrespect, we become self-destructive instead of recognizing what is *really* going on. We stuff our emotions and turn on ourselves, believing on some level that we deserve to be treated poorly.

When events happen that cause you to suffer, your internal critic may put the blame on you. Chances are it believes that berating you will be the motivating force to take you to a place of perfection, thus preventing painful experiences from ever occurring again. The problem is that your attempts to be perfect do not protect you from the aggressive acts of other people, nor do they save you from the unavoidable suffering of life.

An internal critical voice directed at your body is an expression of fear that can prod you to try to change it in some way, promising that doing so will solve all of your problems. This thinking process diminishes life force; it leaches away joy and does nothing to improve your physical or emotional health. And many people find that even if they do get closer to or achieve their "ideal" body, life is still life, and suffering inevitably occurs.

In my own life, fear of being humiliated was a primary reason for being so cruel to myself. Childhood experiences with classmates had left me with the conviction that being perfect was the ultimate protection. If I had a "perfect" body, I would rise above the bullying and sexual harassment that was happening at school. If I never said anything "wrong," no one would tease me.

Looking back I can see that my young self thought perfection would make me invisible. Consequently, any time I didn't "get it right" I felt shame. Even in the most trivial situations, out came the whip. Some part of my brain believed this self-inflicted pain would teach me a lesson. But it is no surprise that treating myself in this way only caused suffering. My misguided trust in my critical voice—in fear's voice—led to the drastic behaviors that nearly killed me in my attempts to lose weight and perfect my body.

Many of us are inducted into the ritual of body bashing at an early age. We cut ourselves down when we compare our bodies to societal images and to other people in our lives. This practice is often unconscious; we learn to do it because we are taught to do so by those around us and by the media we ingest. Sadly, few of us learn during our formative years to relate to our bodies with love and appreciation.

Adolescents and teens (and these days even young children) spend endless hours thinking about or attempting to transform their bodies to look like societal idols. Through this process, many learn to sharpen their negative voice until it cuts like a knife, wounding them severely with self-criticism. As adults, the negative voice practiced in childhood can become so deeply internalized that we forget there was a time in life when it did not exist. It becomes unconscious, which is much more dangerous. I spent years turning other people's judgments, criticisms, and dislike of me into my own internal monster; I hurt myself more than anyone else ever could.

If the monster's voice is allowed to continue to berate us year after year, we end up believing something is innately wrong with us—not only with our bodies, but also with the way we are living our lives. We may think other people are better than we are or more "together." In order to improve our self-esteem, we strive to present a perfect image to the world through our bodies, clothes, homes, careers, or children. This striving for a state of perfection can feel like running on a hamster wheel, spinning endlessly round and round in our perceived inadequate state, never reaching a destination. We lose peace. We lose love for our precious selves. Our critical voice runs rampant, clouding our vision of who we truly are and why we are here. Life force is diminished; purpose and joy are lost.

It is not always easy to resist the voice that tells us we're flawed. Don't forget that advertisers give us just this message so we will spend our money attempting to fix ourselves. There is a reason the diet industry generates about sixty billion dollars per year! The fear-promoting messages seep in if we are not vigilant in our fight for self-love.

TOOLS FOR QUIETING THE CRITICAL VOICE

"You can search throughout the entire universe for someone who is more deserving of your love and affection than you are yourself, and that person is not to be found anywhere. You, yourself, as much as anybody in the entire universe, deserve your love and affection."

—The Buddha

The ultimate goal is to find compassion for our critical voices, honoring that they are often protective mechanisms that shield the parts of us that are easily hurt or humiliated. These defense mechanisms most likely came to us when we were young and unable to turn away from fear. And they will only become quiet when they know we are committed to taking care of ourselves, which means we must be steadfast on our journey towards self-love.

One of my protectors was a voice that said I was stupid. It incessantly told me to keep my mouth shut so I wouldn't embarrass myself. I learned to have compassion for the voice only when I understood that it arose to protect me from humiliating myself by sharing my most vulnerable parts. As my self-love grew I was able to thank this voice for trying to keep me safe when I was too young to discern with whom to share my intimate self. The practice I developed to quiet my critic was to imagine being in a classroom and asking it to go to the back of the room, put its head down on the desk, and take a nap—a very long nap! I saw it as a child who was acting out, but who was really just tired and afraid and needed time to rest. I explained that my self-love was keeping vigil.

Though we may intellectually understand that self-love is a valuable quality to possess—offering us what we need for self-preservation while also expanding our capacity to love others—it can still be elusive. Wouldn't it be nice if we just made the decision to have self-love and *voilà*, it stayed with us for the rest of our lives! I used to think something was wrong with me when moments of peace and trust in myself were followed by nasty comments from my critical voice. Thinking I was supposed to be done with self-criticism (ha-ha!), I would even berate myself for berating myself! This cycle gave me the same feeling as looking at a funhouse mirror where the image goes on into infinity; I thought the mean voice in my head would last forever.

My understanding of suffering and the true meaning of self-love expanded when I spent seven days at a Vipassana meditation retreat. Through the teachings of the Buddhist monk and a week in silent practice I learned that suffering comes and suffering goes, peace comes and peace goes. In the moments when I could still my active mind, I was able to detach from the grasping need to control my experiences. Many times throughout the week I felt on the brink of madness, absolutely certain I was going to explode from the painful thoughts and feelings spinning in my brain. And then I would practice mindfulness, paying attention only to each breath going in and out of my nose during sitting meditation, or taking one small step followed by another in walking meditation. Stillness inevitably followed. I became aware of a nonjudgmental observer entering my psyche, one that viewed all of the thoughts and feelings that drifted through my brain without attachment to any of them.

In the years that followed, I came to know that I am not served by trying to hold on to any emotions or experiences—even the "good" ones. I can't force positive feelings to stay, just as I can't force my critic to leave forever. What I can do is breathe, come back to the moment whenever possible, and trust in the impermanence of things, including all feelings. When I forget and become attached to outcomes, my critical voice speaks up and I suffer. Through much practice, however, I've become adept at forgiveness, which means I no longer beat myself up for being self-critical.

I find that my most profound experiences of self-love are in moments of stillness, when I am detached from ego and striving. We do not find self-love by searching through our minds; we can't intellectualize our way there. It is found in the quiet places, in our breath. When we are capable of quieting our minds, we can enter into a heart space, breathing through whatever is occurring in the moment. Even the most difficult experiences become easier when we let our minds take a step back and create room for our hearts to lead.

I had a conversation recently with my friend Jessica Diaz (a Body Positive leader since her teens and now a board member of our organization) about what it means to have a self-loving internal observer. At our dinner together, we shared stories about how active our critical voices had been lately, and how our compassionate observers kept us conscious of self-criticism as it was happening. These witnesses made it possible to remember that there were lessons in the struggles we were experiencing. Even though our minds were running rampant with unkind thoughts, self-love let us hear these critics, yet protected us from thinking we had to act in accordance with their wishes. We used the experiences to recognize where we were out of balance, and where messages from the outside world had seeped in to cause our suffering. Through this process, our negative voices—our fear—eventually quieted, allowing us to make conscious attitudinal and behavioral shifts that brought back our joy.

ELIZABETH

LOVE

In Buddhist thought, the cultivation of *metta*—love—is the first of the four foundations on the path to liberation from suffering. Love is not a quality we have to create inside of ourselves; it is the practice of uncovering and experiencing the basic goodness we already possess. Buddhism teaches us to harness this inexhaustible power of love to overcome fear, separation, and despair.

Even though our critical voices never go away completely, we *can*, through practice, build a foundation of self-love that lessens the severity of their impact on our lives. We may encounter obstacles—painful childhood experiences, loss, or trauma, for example, can hinder our ability to hold on to kindness towards ourselves. If the idea of loving yourself seems impossible, you'll want to seek help from an outside source, such as a therapist, spiritual guide, or friends and/or family members.

The techniques I described are a few of the many ways to connect with self-love. The remainder of this section offers further tools for practice.

embody

Choose Love

"I got an email out of the blue from a random listserv at school about The Body Positive that suggested the idea of self-love. It seemed fantastic and crazy at the same time, like who would have thought you could actually love yourself? Connie and Elizabeth were the first people I met who truly loved themselves. They talked about what they were trying to do to teach others to have self-love, but they also role modeled it. I could believe their words because they were exuding their own love for themselves. How could I not believe that?"

—Lily S., Body Positive leader

An essential element of building a practice of self-love is recognizing that *we have the power in every moment to choose love over fear.* Though we may have negative conditioning from our past to overcome, by making the decision over and over again that we are worthy of our own love, the practice gets easier. In each moment, it is absolutely possible to choose love. Though it may slip away immediately, through conscious attention you keep making the choice, and—in time—your life transforms. Eco-philosopher Joanna Macy explains our power to choose in this way: "Since a person's actions derive from her unique observations and reflections, she can always choose. Though her reactions are conditioned by previous experience, present circumstances bring ever-new perceptions and opportunities." [8]

Fear's voice is enticing because it can sound so logical. *If I just change this or that about myself, then everything in my life will be easier.* Acting from a place of fear, however, generally leads to short-term changes only, with false promises of solutions to all of our problems. It tends to cause impulsive actions, or it does the opposite—paralyzes us.

Love opens us to our innate wisdom; it is steady. Choosing to listen to love's voice keeps us in the present moment, where decisions can be made and behaviors enacted that lead to positive, life-enhancing outcomes. Instead of going on a diet as fear may insist, love prompts us to reach into our hearts for what will bring us true nourishment, joy, and vitality.

I had an experience many years ago where I was in conflict with a man whose actions made my life extremely difficult. It felt at the time like self-love was gone forever. My critical voice was relentless, telling me the situation was my fault; if I weren't such a passionate, emotional, outspoken creature, the dispute would never have happened in the first place. I could only hear fear speaking to me. After weeks of suffering, I drove into a parking spot in a public garage one evening and looked up to see the following graffiti spray painted on the wall above my car:

LOVE YOURSELF!
If you don't, who will?

This message was all it took for me to quiet my critical voice and fill me with gratitude for the unknown person who had stated so simply what I was struggling to reach on my own. A switch flipped in my brain and my suffering ended on the spot. Days later, I learned that a friend who had been battling lung cancer would not win her fight for life. It was news that put my self-inflicted suffering into perspective: the ultimate reminder that if I choose to listen to fear's voice, I am wasting the most precious gift I have been given—life itself.

From this experience I was able to recognize that the traits that led me into the conflict served me well in other parts of my life—especially my work. I honored myself for being passionate, emotional, and outspoken, and stepped away from the conflict with my wholeness and belief systems intact. I chose to listen to love over fear, and my suffering ended.

When your critical voice speaks up to tell you you're ugly, stupid, unworthy, etc., that is the moment to recognize fear talking and do whatever you can to get back to love. One way I transform fearful energy is by saying the word "love" over and over again in my head. This practice offers love a chance to penetrate my psyche. I can actually sense my body soften and relax immediately just from saying the word. I may still have further work to do to quiet my critic, but this action is great for getting the process started—and keeping it going.

Not everyone responds to verbal messages. We hear a variety of constructive options from people who attend our workshops and lectures. Some are able to move from fear to love by thinking of others who love them just as they are (e.g., partners, children, siblings, parents, grandparents, friends, pets). Others have said they experience love by thinking about a particular place where they feel (or once felt) good about themselves (e.g., a favorite place in nature, a special vacation spot, a childhood home, their grandmother's lap). They go to this place in their mind's eye and their mean voice lessens in intensity. Many people use prayer or meditation to silence their inner critic. Others say that using their bodies physically, especially to move through nature, quiets the monster inside. I have also found humor to be a good friend when I'm searching for a loving voice to replace my fearful one.

ANONYMOUS

BODY POSITIVE WORKSHOP PARTICIPANT AND VOLUNTEER

As a sophomore in high school I began to foster an interest in eating nutritious foods and living a healthy lifestyle. However, my positive intentions slowly evolved into an obsession and I developed an eating disorder.

I felt very alone during my high school years. I did not know how to deal with my feelings; I thought I needed to change. It was never my intention to hurt myself; I just wanted a happier life, my vision of which was highly influenced by societal messages convincing me that I needed to be thin to be happy and healthy. The more I tried to educate myself about nutrition and health, the more I became obsessed with numbers: calories, weight, ounces of meat, slices of bread, etc. These obsessive behaviors continued into my first semester of college, when I realized I needed support.

Shortly after reaching out, I attended my first Body Positive workshop. It sincerely helped turn my life around. Connie and Elizabeth's voices spoke to my heart. Their self-love radiated out and imbued my own self-love. Author Stephen Buhner explains this phenomenon: "When a person projects a heart-coherent field filled with caring, love and attention, living organisms respond to the information in the field by becoming more responsive, open, affectionate, animated, and closely connected."[9]

My disordered eating did not change overnight, however. My recovery is an ongoing process; I continue to feel more myself, little by little. As I look back, I realize that my initial notion to change myself was rooted in an innocent fear—fear of loneliness and social rejection. This fear silently created an expanding abyss in my thoughts. In doing so, it dissolved the fragile net of love that was previously interwoven into my life. I received messages of love as a younger child, but messages of self-love seemed to stop as I grew older. Nobody ever sat down with me and had an earnest conversation about loving myself, especially as my body began to change. As a result, exploring self-love is a pivotal focus of mine during my healing process.

For me, practicing self-love means living from my heart. One thing I like to do is imagine what my heart wants or needs and then do my best to create whatever that may be. This act of "listening and giving" is self-loving. The process can take minutes or months.

I am learning to listen to my heart over and over again, like exploring an infinite set of Russian nesting dolls. Each choice to follow my heart and deepen my self-love is like opening another doll. Thus far I have made the bigger choices, the outermost dolls. These include my initial reach out for help, a break from school, and my pursuit of farming. In this infinite set of Russian nesting dolls, the choices to follow my heart will never end.

Resist Aggression

"The way to transform this world is to speak truth to power, and we start by speaking to the critical voice inside ourselves. Self-love stands up to the critical voice and transforms it from fear into vulnerability. Our willingness to embrace vulnerability leads to openhearted, authentic living."

—Elizabeth Scott

One way in which people combat negative feelings about themselves is to harness the natural energy of their anger into a protective force to resist aggression. A perfect story to illustrate this point comes from a teen who participated in our first Body Positive leadership program. She was facilitating her high school discussion group one day and told the following story to her peers:

"My dad was yelling at me last night, and as I sat there listening to him, I looked down at my thighs and saw them getting bigger. I heard Elizabeth's voice say, 'If this wasn't about your body, what would it be about?' and I suddenly realized there is nothing wrong with my thighs. They are just fine. The problem is my dad's a dick!"

The room filled with a nervous twitter as the other students processed the meaning of this honest message, which can be translated as:

There is nothing wrong with my body. The outside world is sometimes out of my control and makes me unhappy. I don't have to hate myself. I can feel anger towards people and situations that are hurtful. I have a choice in how I feel about and talk to myself. I can protect myself by setting boundaries. It's okay to resist the real aggression in my life by holding people accountable for their actions instead of focusing on improving myself and hoping this will change the actions of others.

Our young leader's lessons are many: life's troubles are not always about our bodies; perfecting our appearance will not make problems disappear or cause people to stop saying mean things to (or about) us; and, in the face of aggression, we must do the best we can to express our truth, and reach out for support when this is not possible.

It helps to first recognize acts of aggression. We tend to think of these as "in your face," which they can be, but they can also be as subtle as someone giving your body the once-over with their eyes when they greet you, or a friend talking about another friend's body in a disparaging way. And the experience might have nothing to do with your body, as was the case with our young leader.

I find that aggressive acts affect me physically. My body will start to lightly shake all over, or I'll feel a heaviness in my gut that lets me know I'm not okay with what has just taken place. There is no "right" way to respond to our aggressors. The voice we use might be one of anger, love, or some other emotion. If speaking is not a safe option, we reach inside for a fierce quality of love to protect us from turning the harmful words of others into a critical voice of our own, or into self-destructive behaviors. We work to find the clarity needed to know the hostile act of another person is not our fault, and that we are allowed to keep our self-love intact. If necessary (and possible), we ask someone to speak for us when we are disempowered by someone's hurtful act. It is important to reach out for help if you are repeatedly harmed by the words or actions of others and don't have the skills or option to resist.

One form of aggression we all deal with is the onslaught of imagery and messages from advertisements made by the people and corporations that profit from our self-criticism. These are purposely created to lead us into believing that transforming ourselves will make us acceptable and loveable. The ways in which we are to mold ourselves are dictated to us by what I call the big, nebulous *they* out in the world. We sacrifice our internal wisdom with the hope that if we follow *their* edicts (which are forever changing) more strictly, true love, great success, and unconditional acceptance will be ours. Since it's hard to get an audience with the advertising executives who do everything in their power to manipulate our thinking, we must remain alert in order to reject their messages that aim to cause our suffering.

A subtle form of aggression most of us experience regularly is being around people who criticize themselves. Though their intention is not to hurt us with their words (only themselves), listening to negative self-talk can seep in and make us feel that something is wrong with our own bodies or lives. Choosing to make positive statements about ourselves in these situations is not easy to do but absolutely worth the effort. Silence can also be a great protector. Refusing to join in makes a powerful statement. The self-critical people we're with may become more aware of their own voices. If not, at least we're not bashing ourselves. If I can't change the conversation, I find it helpful to simply walk out of the room.

My daughter developed a highly creative tool for resisting aggression when she was in the fourth grade. It is one I have used many times myself and share with people of all ages. A girl in Carmen's class was extremely mean to her because she felt competitive about who was smarter. Carmen wasn't participating in this competition; she was just enthusiastic about learning. The girl put a note on her chair that said, "I hate you, Carman" (even misspelling her name in the hate note!). Carmen was hurt, yes, but she didn't absorb the girl's message. She had no intention of changing herself to be liked by this girl. Her self-love remained intact. I asked her how she was able to so easily fend off hurtful comments from others. Her response was, "I just don't take it in, Mom."

"But how?" I asked, hoping she could teach me a skill I did not at that time possess. "What exactly do you do in your mind to stop the comments from getting into your body?"

"Well," she began, "I imagine turning my back to the person, and on my back is a mirror. The mean thing they said is reflected back and doesn't make them feel very good. My tummy is like a soft pillow. When people say nice things to me I take them into the soft, squishy pillow and I feel really good!" While speaking this last sentence her arms were wrapped around her belly in a hug, and a radiant smile lit up her face.

Needless to say, I was floored. My nine-year-old daughter possessed a protective skill I was still searching for at forty. Where was my mirror in grade school, junior high, and high school when kids were mean to me? Why was I not able to absorb loving comments into a squishy pillow in my belly? And why was I still, as a middle-aged woman, absorbing negativity from the outside world into my cells when so much around me was positive? *Because I was still in the process of understanding that true self-love was possible for me just as I was, with all of my perceived imperfections.* Though I had healed my relationship with my body, I was still grappling with the need for perfection in other areas of my life. Carmen's story gave me a brilliant tool for keeping the negative voices from the outside world right where they belong—with the people who say mean things! Her words helped me take a quantum leap forward in my quest for freedom from my internalized critic.

Carmen is now a young woman, and I see that the skills she developed to deflect the mean comments of her peers protected her from internalizing the type of nasty, critical voice I hear in most people. She is human, of course, and has days when she is unkind to herself, but I've never known anyone who can so easily move past self-critical moments to get back to her self-love.

Practice Forgiveness

Forgiveness is a crucial ingredient for living with self-love. We are human. We don't always do or say things "correctly." We make what we consider "mistakes," and get ourselves into difficult situations. At the meditation retreat I mentioned earlier, I learned a simple yet powerful forgiveness meditation that has stayed with me ever since:

> *If by deed, speech, or thought, foolishly I have done wrong*
> *All forgive me Honored Ones*
> *Who are in wisdom and compassion strong*
> *I freely forgive anyone who may have hurt or injured me*
> *I freely forgive myself*

I recite these words regularly as they gently remind me that even though my intentions stem from my heart, I may still *foolishly* blunder and create suffering for myself or other people. This meditation quiets the obsessive message swirling around in my brain telling me I'm bad for making a mistake. And it reminds me that love is what ultimately matters. I am able to make amends when necessary—with others or myself—and turn my attention back to what is truly important in my life.

ELIZABETH

SELF-LOVE IN RELATIONSHIPS

Self-love is one of the essential tools I give my clients to help them in relationships. When you are in a difficult moment in relationship with another person, it is helpful to remember that you are worthy of love even when you have made what you think is a "mistake," even when you are so confused that you don't know how to repair the damage caused by your actions or words. In these moments, you have an opportunity to reach deeply into your heart and remember that you are capable of love. Remind yourself that you are willing to learn something new from the problems you and your partner are having. Stay open to finding out what the difficult moment is about. If you take the time to express what is true for each of you and speak directly from your hearts, you can work out your difficulties. And if your struggles are too monumental to overcome, your self-love will give you strength to go separate ways.

When you collapse into self-loathing, thinking you're bad for whatever has caused the conflict, you have no resources to contribute to healing the situation. If you fall back on your self-

---

love, though, you remember that even if it takes time to figure out the struggle, you are still a good person who is capable and worthy of love. You have the resources to patiently try to understand your partner's point of view and also figure out your own part in the struggle. Staying with self-love keeps you from withdrawing your love from your partner. You don't need to prove they are wrong in order to feel good about yourself.

I teach my couples clients to focus on what they need to say to each other instead of being sidetracked with concern about their own worth and value as people. It's distracting to be preoccupied with *I'm not good enough* or *I'm a bad person* in the middle of a communication issue. It's much more useful to focus on the conflict at hand rather than being in your own struggle about how you're inadequate. When you and your partner both cultivate the deep sense of worthiness that comes with self-love, you bring unlimited resources to your relationship—resources that are especially useful during the inevitable difficult moments.

I was taught during my upbringing that being a hero was about doing big brave deeds in the world. What I have learned as a mother and a partner is that love takes bravery. During the hard times, I must be fierce with myself to avoid collapsing into criticism. Self-love allows me to stay centered in my self-worth, forgive myself, and learn whatever lesson I am meant to learn. The courage this requires then expands my capacity to give and receive love. What a useful resource!

Think about how deepening your self-love might help you in all types of relationships (with partners, friends, children, family, and work colleagues). Build your practice and see if it helps you become a better communicator; it is the warrior's path to reach for the equilibrium of self-love rather than collapsing or attacking in relationships. I believe no pursuit is more important than this.

LYNN SCOTT

ELIZABETH'S MOM

I stopped hating my body in my seventy-fifth year. I'd made many attempts to love it, and I'd succeeded in the past, for brief times...

I'd been a happy tomboy in the 1940s, beginning menses late and having no shape till almost college. I felt betrayed when all that began. College dorms were the dressing rooms for torture: brassieres and underarm pads, waist pinchers, long-leg girdles and stockings that attached to either the girdles or a garter belt that hung below the waist with four pincher clips to hold them up. During "the curse" (as our mothers had called menstruation), we added silly, thin, elastic Kotex belts that had a back and front fastener with teeth that were supposed to hold the pad between our legs.

In those days, we girlfriends didn't discuss anything that I have just written. And we never talked about what was happening to our bodies. This unnatural squelching of my development into young womanhood, added to by cryptic asides from my equally suppressed mother, "I know you would never do anything to hurt me dear" (the only sex education I received), lay the path to my alienation from my healthy body.

I married, had four children, was divorced, and fell into the feminist second wave with abandonment. Yet I didn't feel like a woman—amazing, eh? It was when I was forty-four years old at a speculum party and saw all those vaginas, beautiful in their stages of life, just like mine, when I finally accepted that I was a woman. I had already abandoned the entrapments of half the undergarments of my early adult days, but shame still hung on my thighs. For a long time, I just covered it over.

Certainly the women's community, with its focused music, talking circles, openness about love in all forms, gave us opportunities to carry our voices out against the Vietnam War, racism, civil rights. I found a platform to leap off into graduate school, a non-traditional counseling collective of bright men and women. We knew that power over anyone was the same old rift we'd been subjected to as women.

By the time I was fifty-six, I was once again alone after two serious attempts at marriage, one that gave me my children, and another with a woman. As I've said, there were periods of time, especially within my second relationship, where I accepted my body based on how much it was loved by my partner. However, the complex damage of my upbringing, and of hers, sent me fleeing after ten years.

I was a mother as well as a grandmother when my own mother died and I inherited my eighty-year-old father. My son, long a troubled boy and now a troubled man, was my focus, too, between my fifty-sixth and seventieth years. All my energy was turned outwards. I still founded women's organizations to support up-and-coming talented women, yet there was inner work to do.

I attended Quaker Meetings throughout my adult life, knew the value of meditation, and had an early connection with Spirit.

But I'd misplaced the power of that inward journey. The same year I lost a breast to cancer I found Spirit Rock, a Buddhist meditation center, and a somatic experiencing counselor who wouldn't accept my talking head. She led me into the unknown realm of my body feelings. For years I had written everything I could about my family of origin—the good and the bad—but now I had learned to recognize that the dramas my mind delivered endlessly were separate and quite irrelevant compared to the long-held feelings sitting heavily in my body.

It has come to me at last that while suffering seems to be the name of the game on planet earth, there are steps one can take to embrace it all. By not dodging or denying, by taking the time to be with myself at my core, by working on putting out loving kindness towards myself as well as those within my circle and everything live, I am quite content in this "overweight," single-breasted body that seems to be far older than I am. I will give it the same love as it ages that I gave my father into his nineties. This is freedom and personal power at last.

SOWING SEEDS OF SELF-LOVE

"When I learned to love my body, I learned to love all that my body is capable of doing and enduring. I learned that this body will change and grow and age with me. It is mine to enjoy, adorn, love, protect, and present to the world. It is a gift inherited from my family, and it is my responsibility to love and cherish it."

—Jessica Diaz, The Body Positive board member

"Self-love is not for sissies!" said Elizabeth to a group of New Yorkers during a 2011 Body Positive workshop. She was right—and the participants in our workshop agreed. It is not an easy feat to have self-love in a world that pushes us to amplify our inadequacies (just look at the magazine covers as you're standing in line at the grocery store) and calls us mean names when we say out loud that we love ourselves. It is much easier to blame our bodies, lives, or other people for our problems, and to release responsibility for our own contentment.

Elizabeth and I view the work of cultivating self-love as one of the most important tasks people can undertake. Just as self-loathing and body dissatisfaction can color every aspect of your life, so can self-love. Choosing it is like committing to a loving relationship. There are rough patches, of course, but the rewards are endless. Living with self-love demands that you repeatedly dig deep inside to understand that you deserve to cherish yourself, just as you would cherish a partner, dear friend, or child.

Your body does not have to be the cause of your suffering. You might try thinking of it as the amazing vehicle that allows you to move through this world, or a vessel to be filled with life's rich experiences. Each and every one of us has unique gifts to offer, which are meant to be shared. When we stop blaming our bodies for our struggles, we have an unlimited capacity to use our talents to make the world a better place, even in the smallest of ways.

Cultivating self-love is like planting a garden. Both take time and effort, especially as you get started. Preparing your soil can be hard work, and planting seeds can be tiring. For some time, nothing happens. You have a plot of dirt that needs attention, but you don't see any results of your labor. Then, abruptly, little plants push their way through the ground and begin their journey towards the sun. Day by day they get bigger, and soon you see flower buds begin to form. Your garden continues to require attention and care, but suddenly your flowers bloom and you are rewarded with vibrant beauty and abundant joy. Your vegetable and fruit plants turn their flowers into food that sustains your life. So it is with self-love. It takes more time and attention in the beginning, but one day you wake up and realize that tending to your self-love garden has become part of your every day life—and you blossom. You are rewarded with a bountiful crop: a balanced relationship with your body, freedom to pursue your dreams and purpose, a deepened connection to the people in your life, and more beauty surrounding you than you ever imagined possible.

This analogy might not work for you. If that is the case, think about what you *do* like to do. Are you a musician? Do you practice your instrument regularly, knowing that when you first attempt to play a new song it probably doesn't sound great? With time and practice, though, the song reveals itself through your instrument and you experience the beauty of listening to the results of your creativity and hard work. Perhaps you like to do jigsaw or number puzzles. In the beginning, there is no order. With attention and patience, however, the pattern reveals itself and everything fits into place. As you do more puzzles, they become easier to solve and you search out more challenging ones because your brain is rewarded when you find the solutions. If you are a dancer, you know the joy of practicing a physical movement repeatedly. Over time, you put many movements together and can perform an entire dance, bringing delight to both you and your audience. Think about what *does* feed your soul, and use it as inspiration to put the same attention, practice, patience, and care towards enhancing your self-love.

I invite you to explore the ideas and practices in this chapter to find the tools that work best to help you to step towards self-love and away from self-criticism, even when those around you choose to partake in this fruitless ritual. Remember that loving yourself takes practice—and courage. The more you use your gentle, compassionate voice, the faster your brain will recognize this new pattern and more easily respond with loving kindness instead of an attack from your nasty critic. Self-love is your ultimate protection.

BODY POSITIVE PRACTICES

Giving Yourself Permission

As you cultivate self-love, you become aware of how you want to treat yourself and be treated by others. You also become more closely connected to your life purpose and the values by which you wish to live. It takes courage and the willingness to take risks to live from this place. The practice offered here is to help you give yourself permission to follow your heart.

INSTRUCTIONS

Sit or lie down in a comfortable position. Breathe in and out and allow your body to become quieter with each breath. Notice any thoughts that are in your brain, and, without judgment, allow them to pass through. From this quiet place, explore any sanctions or restrictions that block you from living fully, from expressing your true purpose, your creativity, your unique gifts. What is in the way of treating yourself kindly? Of being treated how you would like by others? These obstacles might come from outside sources, such as the parameters of your job or the voice of someone who tells you how you *should* live your life. Or, they may be inside your own mind, fears that block you from having the life experience you desire. Allow yourself as much time as you need to observe what comes up.

When you're ready, get your journal or a piece of paper and write at the top of the page, "I give myself permission to..." Now, without consciously thinking too much, write down everything that comes to mind. What do you want to give yourself permission to do? For example, "I give myself permission to notice my critical voice when it comes up, and to explore why it's being mean to me" or, "I give myself permission to express my creativity by signing up for a painting class."

Some people feel that they're not ready to give themselves permission to do or have what they want, so they head their paper with, "I *want* to give myself permission to..." Do this practice in whatever way feels most useful. Remember, this is for you only, so let yourself be free to write down even the most outlandish things. You'll know you're done when your hand stops writing and your brain feels still. Give yourself time to look over the list to see which items you want to take on first. These might be the easiest, or the ones that ignite the most passion when you read them.

Make a new permission list whenever you find that you're stuck in a behavioral or attitudinal rut, need to make a big decision, or are giving yourself a hard time for one reason or another. It's a great way to gather information from your inner wisdom.

Moving from the Critical Voice to Self-Love

Your critical voice, though not very pleasant, offers an excellent opportunity for you to find out what you're afraid of, face your fear, and give yourself the gift of reaching for self-love. This practice takes you through a process of having a dialogue with your critical voice, followed by a meditation that will help you give yourself unconditional love. Note: I recommend not doing the work with your critical voice unless you have time to do the whole practice.

INSTRUCTIONS

a. **Talking with Your Critic:** Think for a moment about how your critical voice has been speaking to you lately. It might sound like, "You're not..." or, "Why can't you..." or, "I'm too..." or, " If only you'd..." (fill in the blank). The exact form it takes will be unique to your life experience. Write down the statement that comes to mind, or, if there are many, one in particular that you'd like to work on right now.

embody

Now, have a dialogue with your critic to learn more about what it is afraid of and what it actually needs. Take time to think about and write your answers to the following questions. Don't over-think your responses; let your inner critic speak honestly.

- Critical voice, if you are just fear talking, what are you afraid of?

- What do you need to feel less afraid?

- How would you feel if you got what you needed? For example, peaceful, confident, brave, relieved, competent, content, etc.

Whatever it is that your critical voice is trying to attain, this is the internal resource you will want to reach for. Take time to think or write about what it would feel like to give yourself an abundance of this nourishing resource—in this very moment.

- Can you take the risk to have more (peace, confidence...) in ways that don't include trying to change the size or shape of your body?

b. **Reaching for Self-Love:** This part of the practice offers a meditation to explore what it feels like to move into a deep place of self-love. It is not a place of perfection you get to and stay, but a practice you cultivate that can be used as a response when your critical voice starts to speak. Do this meditation as often as necessary—and in whatever way works best for you—to remember that *you can always reach for love.* Alternatively, you can reach for the internal resource that came up in the preceding "Talking with Your Critic." Doing so will also enhance your experience of self-love, because you're giving yourself what you need in the moment.

Sit or lie down, and close your eyes, if you choose. Adjust your body to get as comfortable as possible. Feel the support of the beautiful, nourishing earth beneath you. Breathe deeply into your body, and imagine every one of your cells now receiving the oxygen they need to thrive. Let your breath flow into all parts of your body, starting with your head and moving down to your toes. Observe the places where you are holding tension. You don't have to do anything except observe what is happening in your body in this moment.

Remind yourself that you are a part of the whole of creation, and, like every other living thing, you deserve to be nourished. Feel the rhythm of your breath going in and out and allow yourself to sink into the supportive and generous earth. Now, use your imagination to create a safe space for you to enter here and now. Imagine that this space is filled with a never-ending abundance of unconditional love. In this loving space, all aspects of your body, soul, and spirit are cherished, including your perceived flaws and imperfections. You may visualize an actual physical place, or it may be one you make up in your imagination. Wherever it is, this place is here for you always. You may see it in your mind's eye, or it might just be a feeling of comfort and safety that you experience. Stay here as long as you'd like.

Now, feel the shelter and warmth of the brilliant sky above you. The sky offers you the oxygen you breathe, the sunlight required for life on earth, and asks nothing in return as it gives you its life-giving gifts. Allow this protective and tender love to envelope you. Feel yourself centered right here in the middle between the loving and generous earth and the tender and protective sky.

Here you are...perfectly made and lovingly cherished. This place is always here for you whenever you need to feel love for yourself. The natural world never judges, never criticizes, never excludes. It offers unconditional love in ample abundance. Its beauty is always available to show you your true reflection. Reach deeply into your heart and open to the love and compassion that are always waiting there, even when you forget. Find time as often as possible to connect with this loving space. Take a deep breath that once again reaches every cell in your body. When you're ready, come back to the room.

Take some time to write about your experience, using the following questions to guide your exploration:

- Was I able to create a safe space in which I accessed unconditional love for myself?

- If not, what obstacles do I need to address to get to this place?

- Am I willing to take the time I need to reach deeply for the nourishing resource of self-love?

- What are specific things I can do on a regular basis to stay in touch with my self-love?

c. **Responding to Your Critic:** In this last part of the practice, you will create a response to your critical voice. On the paper where you held your dialogue with your critic, write one statement about yourself that comes from the unconditional loving voice within you. If you can't access this voice, just pretend there is a person who loves you unconditionally. What would they say about you? Keep this statement with you as a reminder of your truth.

INSTRUCTIONS FOR GROUP PRACTICE

Doing this practice in a safe group setting is extremely powerful. We all have critical voices, so exploring them together, and examining how they affect our relationships with one another, is quite an experience. The instructions are still divided up into three parts, noting when to go back to the individual practice directions for reference.

a. Talking with Your Critic: Sit in a circle. Make sure everyone has a half sheet of blank paper and a pen. Do the first part of the practice the same way as if you're doing it individually, as described before, and have each person write down their critical voice's statement. Now, however, you will all crumple up your pages and throw them into the center of the circle. Mix them up before each person takes one and unfolds it.

The next step is for everyone to get up together and walk around in the middle of the circle reading the critical statements out loud, over and over again. This is an anonymous activity, so even if you get your own, you don't have to say it's yours. After several minutes (someone can be a time keeper), everyone stops moving and reading. As a group, call out your responses to the following questions (read by one person in your group):

- How do you feel in your body right now? What physical sensations do you notice?

- How do you feel in relation to the other people in the room? Connected? Disconnected?

Again, take time to let everyone respond. Go back to your seats and designate one person to go around the room with a recycling bin to collect the crumpled papers with the critical voices written down. Another option is to burn or bury them as a group after you're done with the entire practice.

Have a discussion about what this experience felt like.

- What did it feel like to hear all of the voices at once, out loud?

- How does it make us feel to know everyone has a critical voice? More compassionate towards others? Towards ourselves?

- How do we think having these critical voices running gets in the way of our communication with other people?

Everyone will now do the individual writing activity with their own critical voice. Take about ten minutes for this exploration. As a whole group (or in pairs if your group is large and time is limited) have each person share what they learned about their critical voice, its fears, and the inner resource they really need that their critical voice is trying to get for them, though in a misguided way.

- How can we support one another in taking action to have more of these vital, nourishing resources in our lives?

b. Reaching for Self-Love: Do the meditation as in the preceding individual practice, with one person reading the guided visualization aloud slowly.

c. Responding to Your Critic: Have everyone write down a statement from their unconditionally loving voice inside, as in the "Talking with Your Critic" individual practice. Then, go around the circle and let each person read their statement out loud. Be mindful that this can trigger fears of being labeled conceited or arrogant, so agree in advance that no one will think of others in this way, and that everyone has the right to say kind things about themselves out loud! Have a group discussion about the experience.

- What did it feel like to hear everyone make positive statements about themselves?

- How did it feel to read our own?

- How would our lives be different if we were free to express positive feelings about ourselves from a place of self-love, knowing it's not the same as conceit?

Love Letter

This simple practice is offered to help you see yourself through eyes of love. You're going to write a love letter—to yourself. Some people like to write to an oft-criticized body part (or their whole body if it's the target), first apologizing for criticizing it and then giving it gratitude for all it does each day. The body part can then have its say, expressing whatever comes up.

Other people prefer to write a freestyle letter, allowing their unconditionally loving voice to speak. You might want to write an ode to yourself. Just remember to pick the form of writing that gives you the most joy. If you're struggling to find loving things to say to yourself, imagine that someone who loves you unconditionally is writing the letter, and let them speak.

Consider putting your letter in a self-addressed envelope and giving it to someone with instructions to mail it at a random moment in the future. Or tuck it in a drawer where you'll run across it from time to time. Write lots and lots of these letters to yourself. It's not an act of conceit—it's true self-care!

Loving Touch

Physical affection is one of the ways we remind our close friends and family we love them. It may sound silly, but touching *yourself* with the same care and affection can strengthen your relationship with your body, and feels nice, too! Try petting your elbows or knees like you would a cat, or giving various body parts a tap and a personal hello once in a while. You can stroke your own hair like you would the hair of a loved one, or even nuzzle your own shoulders with your cheek. Massaging your tense spots is a great idea, too, as are self-hugs. These gentle touches can be quick, easy ways to remind you how wonderful it is to have a body, and thank it for being there for you.

COMPETENCY FOUR

Declare Your Own Authentic Beauty

....

GOALS

• Experience beauty as a creative, dynamic process.
• Inhabit your unique body with joy and confidence.

BENEFIT

Expand your imagination to behold authentic beauty in yourself and others.

....

"It seems so obvious that if we really appreciated what a gift it is to be alive in our bodies and how amazingly complex and intricate these bodies are, we wouldn't be able to hate ourselves so well. We would recognize our own beauty not in an arrogant way, but simply as part of the beauty in this amazing world. Just imagine if all the talent in advertising that went into convincing us that we aren't good enough, could be freed for true creative work."

—J. Ruth Gendler, *Notes on the Need for Beauty*

Beauty. It surrounds us in every moment. To me, beauty is the sight of my beloved mother and daughter baking bread together while deep in conversation. It is in the color and fragrance of flowering fruit trees bursting to life in spring; it is my strong, fleshy thighs that carry me easily up imposing granite peaks. I experience beauty in the hug and kind words from a dear friend when I am in pain. It is the light that fills the room at workshops when people recognize their own magnificence.

The fourth Competency of the Be Body Positive Model, **Declare Your Own Authentic Beauty**, addresses the obstacles to seeing your own beauty and invites you to actively participate in experiencing the exquisiteness of our world. There is beauty everywhere, and we are *all* part of it.

We *declare our authentic beauty* by choosing to see and express ourselves just as we are—internal and external qualities combined. Exploring beauty through a Body Positive lens teaches us to have a dynamic, engaged relationship with the world around us. We honor our bodies as we pass through each developmental stage of life, which leads to true self-care, because we don't confuse it with a desire to transform our physical selves to meet someone else's definition of beauty.

When we are blind to our authentic beauty we are more susceptible to harmful societal messages that promote insecurity and doubt. And, as we know, the behaviors that go along with attempts to fundamentally change our bodies can lead us to worse health over time. Seeing our beauty is not an exercise in vanity—it is a necessary component of good physical and emotional health.

My mom uses her morning shower time to thank her body and tell it how wonderful it is. She washes herself with a tender, loving touch, as if she is the child she once was being bathed by the person who dearly loved and respected her. She is eighty-six years old and one of the healthiest, happiest people I know. Her beauty is more radiant every time I see her!

SARAH LEWIN

BODY POSITIVE LEADER

Sometimes I wonder if our cultural obsession with unattainable beauty ideals is a way to make things in life simpler—a sort of cultural defense mechanism. It would be so much simpler if life were only about having the right type of hair, the perfect nose, or the best-fitting jeans. Experiencing beauty in our flaws and strengths—in our ability to control some things and not control others—is a much bigger challenge. Finding beauty in aging, growing, and in being different means beauty is no longer something static we try to attain, but rather a part of our lived, changing experience.

For most of my life, my understanding of beauty, simply put, was a one-dimensional snapshot of someone that was definitely not me. Through a series of moments and relationships, however, my world became broader and less controlled, enabling me to challenge the distorted lens through which my vision was filtered.

One of the most influential of those was my time spent learning and laughing with the women I met at The Body Positive who were living so fully and with so much love that I decided to move across the country to stay near them. These women provided me with the first community where I could experience myself authentically, and where my joy, humor, and fears were not silenced but heard. Within this group I could be entirely myself—my body's story, filled with complexity and contradictions, freckles and curls, was honored and celebrated.

I now see, or rather work on seeing, my beauty in motion. It's not the picture of me mid-laugh, but the actual experience of my laughter. It is me hunched over, my abdominal muscles clenching to the point of pain because I cannot control my giggles. My beauty is visceral. It is in my movements through life; it's my boldness to experience hardship and fear, power and insecurity, kindness and love.

OBSTACLES TO SEEING AND EXPRESSING OUR AUTHENTIC BEAUTY

When we are awake and paying attention, we see beauty everywhere—in nature, art, in other people. So why is it, when it comes to seeing our own, so many of us suddenly become blind? From the one-dimensional "ideal" look created by corporate America, to appearance-based criticism and other formidable social sanctions related to image that begin in childhood and carry over into adulthood, myriad obstacles stand in the way of the beauty that is our birthright. To know true freedom, we must identify and deconstruct any hurtful messages we have received; we must understand how certain experiences may have contributed to the development of an internalized critical voice that perpetuates belief in our ugliness.

Beauty as a Social Construct

Beauty ideals are social constructs, not truth; they only become truth when given that power. One of the ways this happens is if we believe other people have the right to define beauty for us. If we forget that the industries and individuals supplying the imagery profit greatly from excluding us, then we are more susceptible (both consciously and unconsciously) to internalizing their messages and purchasing their products and services.

We can't deny that the glut of "beauty" images we absorb daily has a profound effect on our self-image. Psychologist and author Susie Orbach discusses the power of this imagery on our self-perception in her book *Bodies*. She points out the speed with which adults unconsciously process and match facial expressions and how this influences our reactions to the imagery we see:

> "If we now apply this finding to images which are purposefully coded to be emotionally powerful by evoking mood, solution, aspiration, we realize the inevitability of our almost instantaneous reaction to the torrent of daily and hourly images around us. Many of these images are far from benign. Their purpose is invidious. They are brought to us by the merchants of body hatred." [1]

Looking back through history, we can see that societal "ideal" beauty standards, which have changed over time, tend to leave out the majority of the population. These days—to make matters worse—the images we are bombarded with often show bodies as fragmented parts. We see perfect (perfectly photoshopped) *sections* of bodies; rarely do we see whole people. When we do, they are frequently presented in highly sexualized poses, often with the women displayed in postures submissive to men. Absorbing these images day after day can cause us to become fragmented in our own bodies. Our definition of beauty will then incorporate toned asses, round perky breasts, well-developed six-packs, massive pectoral muscles, jutting hip bones—*disconnected parts*—to the exclusion of other qualities.

People cut themselves into pieces all the time. It's difficult to have a conversation about bodies without hearing comments such as, *My legs are okay, but I hate my stomach. I like my hair, but my legs are too fat. All I want is to have a flat, well-toned stomach. I wish I had bigger muscles in my arms. My arms are too big.* On and on the chopping goes, setting people up to continually compare their bodies with those of others and with the imagery fed to us by the corporations that are after our money. *I want her legs. I want his abs. I want that model's perfect skin. I want anything other than myself*, is what I hear in these statements. *I desire perfection.* Perfection in this case being a computer-enhanced, static image.

No matter how much we improve ourselves, though, we can't replicate the "perfect" people we see in advertising, people who have had every possible "flaw" removed by a Photoshop professional. Even models cannot live up to the images that have been created in their likeness, even after hours of having their hair, makeup, and clothes worked on by stylists. Necks are stretched, dark skin is lightened, waists and thighs are trimmed, breasts are enhanced, abs are better defined. The people who manipulate photos have the final say in defining human "perfection." They generate images that no one can recreate in real life, even if they undergo every cosmetic surgery procedure in the world. We are all flawed, then, because we are living, breathing human beings who can't match the fantasy of the computer technicians. Even people who spend excessive time and money attempting to achieve the "ideal" body will continue to age, their bodies will naturally break down, and any fleeting moment of perceived perfection will be gone. No amount of weight loss or cosmetic surgery will stop any of us from dying—and they may even contribute to our early demise, as was the case with my sister Stephanie.

What people look like to the outside world may not have any influence on their self-perception. Author Naomi Wolf writes of the thousands of diverse readers of her book *The Beauty Myth* who expressed their pain to her because they could not see beauty in themselves:

"There was no common thread that united these women in terms of their appearance: women both young and old told me about the fear of aging; slim women and heavy ones spoke of the suffering caused by trying to meet the demands of the thin ideal; black, brown, and white women—women who looked like fashion models—admitted to knowing, from the time they could first consciously think, that the ideal was someone tall, thin, white, and blond, a face without pores, asymmetry, or flaws, someone wholly 'perfect,' and someone whom they felt, in one way or another, they were not." [2]

Poor self-image is not limited to any particular group of people. In the well-expressed words of Amanda Kessner, who shares her personal story below, "The way we experience our own body image and relate to representations of various bodies differs depending on our social location. Where are we coming from? What is our gender? Our sexuality? Class background? Ability? Cultural heritage? All of these variables affect body image."

AMANDA KESSNER

THE BODY POSITIVE'S OUTREACH COORDINATOR

When I think of myself as a closeted young person, I wonder how my experience would have been different if I had been taught that not everyone is heterosexual, and how I would have felt differently had there been positive representations of queer people and queer woman around me. I remember reading about lesbian experience in a women's studies text book my sophomore year of college. And I remember feeling incredible relief. *This is real*, I thought.

Growing up, it would have been empowering to see myself represented in a positive way. As a queer woman, these positive representations are still few and far between. In a world that places so much importance on visibility and aesthetics, I struggle with both my near absence in the social imaginary and also the blatant misrepresentation of my experience when visible.

I'm not just interested in seeing a stock image of a lesbian woman. I need to see greater representation of the diversity of queer people. I may see images of women that I can more or less relate to, but their assumed heterosexuality is always present. The woman is next to a boyfriend or husband, wearing a wedding ring, subtly communicating that we are not alike.

Part of my healing has been realized with other queer people who know how invalidating it is to be left out of the picture, and with allies who understand how this might feel. I find that having unconditional love for myself feels best. Seeing and honoring what I *am* feels true.

With the proliferation of advertisements promoting an "ideal" look for males as well as females, a rapidly growing number of boys and men also desire to transform their bodies. Some wish to look like the hyper-muscular men in the movies, on TV, and plastered all over men's "health" magazines, but many desire to emulate the emerging styles presented by ultra-skinny male celebrities and models. In one study, 80 percent of both men and women expressed a desire to change their weight, but half of the men wanted to gain while the other half wanted to lose (but still be lean and muscular).[3] A 2007 Columbia University study found that gay and bisexual men are at higher risk for developing eating disorders than heterosexual men.[4] Recent research shows that males constitute 25 percent of people who suffer from anorexia and bulimia and 40 percent of those with binge eating disorder.[5] It is also important to note that most commonly-used assessments to identify eating disorders are biased towards females,[6] and that boys and men do not seek treatment for a number of reasons, including the perceived stigma of having a "women's problem."

I met a young man at a lecture I gave many years ago who was a compulsive over-exerciser. He stood up during the discussion section of my talk to share his distress at his inability to stop working out, even though he was desperate to do so. He had well-toned, large muscles and not an ounce of body fat. He said, "I know I'm not suffering as much as a girl with anorexia, but I just don't know what to do. I can't stop exercising. I've even turned my dorm room upstairs into a gym. What should I do?" I responded by first telling him I didn't believe in a hierarchy of suffering; that his pain was just as real as anyone else's. We talked for a while with the whole group, and then I asked him to speak to me after the session.

He told me in private that he had been, in his words, a "chubby" adolescent and described an experience he'd had in middle school that sent him diving headlong into an exercise compulsion. A friend said his girlfriend only liked him because she felt sorry for him since he was fat. Immediately, the boy began dieting and compulsively exercising, and three years later was unable to perceive his true reflection in the mirror. He said, "I know I'm probably crazy, but, really, I only see fat when I look in the mirror." As he spoke, he was pulling at the part of his shirt that covered his belly.

I described *body dysmorphia* to him, a disorder where people actually cannot perceive the size of their bodies. I told him this had been my experience, too, when I was his age and struggling with my eating disorder. I'll never forget the end of our conversation. Similar to what babies do when they move through an emotional experience, the boy took several shallow intakes of breath followed by a prolonged exhale. With barely contained tears he said, "What you've told me tonight has made all the difference in my life. Thank you."

JULIAN JUAREZ

BODY POSITIVE LEADER

I am who I am: a Latino transgender man. Let me start off by saying that every transgender person has a completely unique story, so mine is as unique as everyone else's. My relationship with my body has been a journey because I have experienced both a female body and now a male body. I did not always know that this was who I was going to become, but deep inside I knew there was something different about me. As a female, it took about twenty years to feel comfortable with my body and love myself for who I was, just me: loud, fat, and proud.

My transition to becoming a man began in college when I learned about the transgender identity. I felt deeply excited and happy that I had found myself once more. Some people expressed the dilemma of, "If you love yourself now, why do you have to change yourself?" My response was, "Yes, I love myself, but for me this transition is going to change my life, spirit, and soul into my true self." It was not going to alter my love for myself, just change my body to feel more like me.

Since beginning my transition I have not looked back. I am very happy with my decision. I could not wait to get pecs with my new body and stroll down the street topless, but that has not happened yet due to my scars. On one hand, I don't go topless for my safety; many transgender people get killed every year just because of who they are. On the other hand, I feel self-conscious and fear being judged. I never thought I would have to go through my insecurities once more, but I am—now as a man.

One thing I learned through The Body Positive leadership training is how to manage my negative inner voice. How I have come to terms with my critic is by recognizing that the judgment is me judging myself, because I can't know what other people are thinking. Everyday, I become a bit braver by not believing my inner critical voice.

I have also become intuitive with my eating habits, and worry more about my health than my actual body image. If I want pecs, with safe exercise they will come—or not—and that is all good. Life is definitely a journey that I am still living through, and everyday is a new challenge. I live with a positive outlook because every minute that I am alive I know I can get to know myself more, and love myself again and again.

Deconstructing beauty ideals and imagery is a necessary task if we wish to expand our imagination enough to behold beauty in ourselves as well as in others. If we wait for magazine editors or advertisers to tell us our particular appearance or lifestyle have suddenly become supreme, we will be lost forever. If we rely on these sources to be our mirrors, we will never see our true reflection. We do not need to turn off the TV forever or never again look at a magazine, but we must *stay conscious* when we are in the presence of imagery and messages intended to reinforce the unkind voices of our internalized critics. We must hoist up protective shields of self-love in these situations, and remember that beauty is so much more than what we are fed by industries that profit from our insecurity.

Social Sanctions That Obstruct
Our Beauty

When we are young, powerful social forces exist that make it difficult (sometimes seemingly impossible) to resist viewing ourselves in a negative light. Many of us do whatever it takes to "fit in," but we lose a part of ourselves in the process—we lose life force.

APPEARANCE-BASED BULLYING

Bullying in the form of physical and/or verbal abuse based on a person's clothing, weight, or other aspects of appearance, has been around for a very long time. It has, however, escalated with proliferation of social media platforms that allow for anonymous, public humiliation. A 2013 survey done by *www.ditchthelabel.org* found that 60.2 percent of the respondents who experienced bullying were targeted for their appearance.[7] These attacks can lead to self-loathing for being different or "wrong," cause social isolation, and affect a person's psychological well-being. There is growing concern among mental health professionals that aggressive forms of appearance-based bullying cause depression, anxiety, eating and exercise disorders, cutting, suicidal ideation, and other problems in young people with low self-esteem—and can even negatively affect those who generally feel good about themselves.[8-9]

One of the great benefits of peer-led Body Positive groups, especially on middle and high school campuses, is that they provide safe environments that break the isolation in which so many people suffer over their bodies. Structured conversations get to the root of the shame and despair students feel, to the underlying causes of imbalances with food and exercise, cutting, and other self-destructive behaviors. Group members learn that their negative self-image is not caused by having the "wrong" body, but by the destructive belief systems about beauty, health, and identity all around them. As a result, they uncover perspective and self-respect—and even self-love.

THE MEAN VOICE

If we remain in isolation with our body shame, without support to deal with criticism from the outside world, negativity directed at us can get buried deep and become an internalized mean voice. Also, if peers, friends, and/or parents are locked into the pursuit of an "ideal" image, their self-critical comments can make us feel that we, too, must put ourselves down for our "flaws." We learn through osmosis that self-criticism is normal.

As an adolescent, I, like many girls, went from being strong and self-assured to feeling that I had to do whatever it took to be accepted by those with more social power. A single experience of being humiliated about the size of my thighs at the age of fourteen exacerbated the shame I felt for having the "wrong" body. By high school, my self-critical voice was alive and well—and extremely outspoken. Recurring sexual harassment added fuel to the fire of my self-loathing; I was absolutely sure that if I were thin enough and behaved "properly" (not having a clue what that meant!), I would be immune from humiliation.

It didn't help that the majority of my friends had perfected the art of body bashing. I will never forget partaking in the grooming ritual in front of a friend's bathroom mirror before heading out to social gatherings. We stood side by side, yet were lost in conversation with our own selves, trashing our physical features. *My breasts are too small. I hate my fat legs. I have too many freckles.* An endless stream of negativity poured from our mouths as we stared at our reflections. I can't remember either one of us ever once saying, *I really like the way my hair looks tonight,* or *I love the way this shirt looks on me,* or anything that resembled a kind word. Every derogatory word uttered during those self-critical moments reinforced, for many years to come, my conviction that I was ugly and in need of physical improvement.

CONFIDENCE CONFUSED WITH CONCEIT

I know very few people who were raised to speak about themselves in a positive light, especially in front of others. What Elizabeth and I have learned in our work with thousands of young people is that any show of confidence, especially when it comes to knowing one's authentic beauty, is judged as conceited. The people who brandish this label have the power to shatter the confidence of others, especially those who are not supported with tools to help them hold on to their self-esteem.

We find it is important to teach people to differentiate between confidence—which is crucial to develop if we are to see and express our beauty—and conceit. The Body Positive's view of these two concepts is this: conceit is competitive, and generally arises out of people's need to mask their insecurities; confident people, however, know their intrinsic value. They are comfortable in their own skin most of the time, and do not need to participate in "one-up" interactions. Nor do they need to judge others to build up their egos. Seeing their own beauty does not stop them from seeing it in others; it allows them to see more.

My daughter Carmen's teenage experience was in direct contrast to mine. During puberty, she and her friends talked about the differences they observed in each other's physical features. Unlike most girls, however, these observations were made while still maintaining love and respect for their own bodies. They not only saw their friends' beauty, but also their own. An outsider might have dubbed them conceited, but they would have been mistaken. What was actually taking place was a rare form of communication among females: girls who actually liked their bodies and were confident enough in their friendships with one another to say so out loud.

SARAH WOLF

BODY POSITIVE WORKSHOP PARTICIPANT

People are like wildflowers in the fields of the world. With water, sun, and nutrient-rich soil, they bloom—folding outwards, expanding, arms reaching towards joy. But sometimes there is wind, punishing rain, hail. Sometimes you are young and have known nothing but life in a bud. Sometimes you are too cold, too torn, too fragile. Sometimes it hurts to bloom.

But this lack of blooming speaks nothing of a flower's worth.

There's a well-intentioned message floating around in our society that self-assurance is more important than physical appearance; you shouldn't worry about your looks as long as you're confident. But what if you haven't learned to love yourself fully and project this to the rest of the world? Are you expected to feel like not enough?

I've sometimes found myself stuck in a cycle of negative thoughts and energy, in which I'm aware that I'm not carrying myself confidently and know that people may be less drawn to me as a result. This awareness drags me into an even lower state of self-esteem: I slouch, I feel bad, I slouch more. But a lack of confidence is no reason to feel shame.

I've learned that forgiveness is key when I feel this way; I give myself permission to love myself even when I don't feel or project confidence. Some days I feel insecure, low-energy, anxious, or downright dissatisfied with myself. And that's okay. I forgive myself for not always celebrating my body, and sometimes dragging it along as if it were a burden and not a gift. I have a budding knowledge inside that I am always beautiful, and that I always deserve love and respect—from myself as well as others. This awareness may manifest itself in my stride as I embody it more—or not. Either way, I deserve respect the way I am. In all states and moods, in all bodily comportments and all stages of achieving self-acceptance, I am brilliant and I am enough.

The Harm of Comparing Ourselves to Others

Though we eventually leave behind the more ritualized social sanctions (as just described) of our formative years, the belief that we need to fundamentally change ourselves to be considered beautiful often endures. Whether our motivation is conscious or unconscious, we continue to mold our behaviors—and bodies—to be "acceptable" to the adult world. We have conversations in which we point out specific physical traits of the person with whom we're speaking, putting ourselves down in the process. We perfect the art of comparison and, with each encounter, end up in a position of superiority or inferiority—and with empty hearts. Many of us feel alone in our suffering. We look out from a scared and lonely place thinking others do not experience the shame we hold in regard to how we look.

It is important to distinguish between the type of comparison that harms all who participate and the simple act of noticing variety in the human race. Observing differences among people is completely natural—children do it all the time as they learn about the world. They may ask why a person is in a wheelchair, or why a person is fat, tall, or has pink hair. When their parents tell them to be quiet and not to stare, they assume that being different is "bad." These admonitions set the stage for judgmental comparison because kids get the sense that the person they are observing is somehow wrong, which is why they are not allowed to look. It is important to teach our children to be respectful in how they observe and interact with people who stand out to them, but we can do it in a way that also explains to them that *difference is simply a part of the world.*

When Elizabeth's daughter Uma was four years old, she commented appreciatively to a fat woman getting out of the pool by saying, "You are round like the moon." The woman, understanding Uma's openness, responded simply by saying, "Yes, I am." My favorite quote from The Body Positive's first *BodyTalk* video project came from Carmen (who was just seven years old at the time) saying, "People who are fat are just the same as people who aren't, but they're just, um, bigger."

PATTY SCHROEDER

CLINICAL PSYCHOLOGIST, HEALTHY WITHIN, INC.

A tall, freckled, sturdy girl growing up in Southern California in the 1980s and 90s, I was painfully aware of the construct of "California beauty." Each summer I tortured my sunscreen-free, Irish skin in the San Diego sun trying to accumulate a decent base tan, because butt-white was not California-pretty. I dieted my way through high school in desperate pursuit of the "beach figure" my body could never achieve. How unfair that it would not conform! As my disordered eating progressed, I got no closer to feeling comfortable in my skin.

Then, one humid August night, I dove into the lake for a swim.

The doctors told me that striking my head on the sandy bottom had broken my spine. At twenty-three, I was quadriplegic. I would never walk again. I might never move my arms again. I was lucky to be alive, they said.

I experienced many losses that day, but there was also an unexpected gift: a shift from obsessing over what my body looked like, to what my body could do. And, at first, it could not do much. My energy was redirected to restoring health and function. Suddenly, the size of my jeans really didn't matter.

The biggest gift of my spinal cord injury was freedom from the notion that my body needed to look a certain way to be of value. Though it had always been true, I could finally accept that no matter what I did, I couldn't possibly look like the women glorified in magazines. I'm not saying I love what I see in the mirror every day...I'm still vulnerable to my inner critic. But now I know that self-care and respect for what my body does will get me closer to relief than deprivation ever did.

When we can honor that diversity exists on every level, we observe difference for what it actually is—just different. We no longer feel the need to compare or judge when we hold this mindset. We can be our real selves without fear because we know that each of us is no better or worse than any other person on the planet. No beauty hierarchy exists, only difference, and we learn to see genuine beauty in ourselves and in all people.

THE NEED TO GRIEVE

"I feel an overwhelming sadness that I have not loved and honored myself and accepted my own body, my own beauty."

—Anonymous

We may feel great sadness after confronting the influences that have made us so self-critical. We may also feel anger (as was my case when I ended my relationship with bulimia) followed by a need to grieve the time we wasted believing in our ugliness. To experience more beauty in life, both in ourselves and in the world around us, it is essential to honor our wounds and to grieve the time during which we were blinded from seeing our true reflection.

I can best illustrate the need for this grieving process by sharing an experience I had in 2001 while co-facilitating a group for middle school girls. Our name was the Girls Empowerment Movement because the acronym GEM perfectly defined the girls, even with their adolescent awkwardness and struggle. During one of our evenings together, the first girl to speak shared a story of the shame she carried because she believed her body was not beautiful. Tears flowed down her cheeks as she talked. The next to speak began to cry as she, too, unloaded her burden of self-loathing. Every single girl in the room began to cry as she revealed her particular story of suffering.

I will never forget the experience of being with these precious young beings as they offered, into our safe space, the pain and tears that stemmed from their belief in their inadequacies: *I'm bigger than all of my friends. My butt is too small. My breasts are too big. I don't have any breasts. People make fun of the color of my skin; they call me yellow.*

At the end of the evening the girls' faces were bright and shiny from crying, yet their souls were lit up like a dazzling show of lightening in a dark sky. It was an electric experience! I will remember for the rest of my days how alive we all were that night. The girls felt genuinely seen and honored through the simple act of sharing their pain within a safe circle of peers and trusted adults. What we witnessed, young and old alike, was the authentic beauty—the essence—that radiates from people when they are given permission to feel love and compassion for their fragile human selves.

The next day it rained incessantly, as if the heavens were crying in pain for the little GEM girls. As I sat on my living room floor watching the deluge outside my window, I could not stop thinking about the outpouring of tears from the night before. I wrote a poem that day dedicated to the girls called *A River of Tears*. I have chosen to share two passages from it because the words remind me that the wounds that diminish our souls' light and limit our ability to see our own beauty are often formed at an early age—a primary reason they are so hard to recognize and heal later in life. The poem was written specifically for the participants in our group, but I believe it speaks to anyone who has been teased, shamed, or humiliated.

A River of Tears

A girl is born
Her spirit a bubbling creek attached to
the deep flowing river that is Mother

Crystal clear and sparkling clean
as her journey begins
she is eventually discovered
Humans want her
and use her innocence
to satisfy their own needs

They leave behind their trash
when they are done
clogging her flowing waters
with their garbage
Pain
Shame
and
Humiliation

build a dam
blocking what was once
free-flowing consciousness

The creek's sparkles dim
Light traveling from the life-giving sun
has difficulty penetrating the layer of smog
that has clouded her spirit
Her soul is buried deep
She is losing form
Life force can no longer find a place to reside
and walks away

The poem continues, telling the story of four women who see the damage done to the creek and set out to clean her waters. The women sing an ancient song about beauty as they step into the murky water to clear trash from the little creek. The sun is setting in deep purple, fiery orange, and soft pink colors when their work is finished. Though the women are tired, their hearts are full.

Suddenly they are aware
of a presence that hovers
at the bank of the little creek
They cannot see her fully
but the women know that
Life
who had walked away
because she could not breathe
was entering the water
ready to once again
give form and beauty
to the little sparkling creek

A new sound is heard
As with the song of the women
this sound begins faintly
and grows to fill
all corners of the evening sky

It is the sound of girls crying
Tears of Pain
Sadness
and
Joy
are released
Cleansing and purifying the girls
as they journey together down
The River of Tears

The girl
The crystal clear sparkling creek
is free once again
from the damaging touch of human hands
Hands that did not see
or care for the precious Gem
The girl
who will someday become
the deep mysterious river
that is Woman

And so we grieve the beautiful moments of life we have lost to feeling inadequate, to seeing ourselves as flawed. We cry a river of tears to honor the wounds we have received at the hands of other humans. When we are done grieving, we willingly step into our own creek to remove the trash that diminishes its sparkling clear waters.

COME HOME TO BEAUTY

"In beauty's presence there is a dignity that is not interior or exterior but coherent. All the way through."
—J. Ruth Gendler, *Notes on the Need for Beauty*

Okay, so you've gotten mad, you've started grieving, and you're ready to do what it takes to clean the garbage from your soul so you can find your beauty. What now? The first thing to remember is that changing the way you see yourself takes practice. Even if you consciously desire to see your beauty, looking in the mirror or seeing your image in a photo or on video may still bring out the mean voice that demands to be heard as it points out all of your "flaws." Don't forget, you may be dealing with deeply-embedded brain patterns that have been around since you were very young: see image of self ... commence criticism ... feel ugly ... act accordingly. It takes commitment, practice, and bravery to include yourself in your definition of beauty.

This section of the chapter and the practices at the end offer ideas, stories, and activities to expand your perspective and bring you home to your beauty. Play with these ideas until you discover the path that is right for *you*.

Make Use of Your Critical Voice

Of course, we all have days when we can't see our beauty. When my critic comes to visit and tells me I'm getting old and wrinkly, or something else is wrong with me that stems from being human, my practice is to recognize the nasty statements as red flags that challenge me to stop and take stock of what is happening in my life. I often find that I am deeply exhausted, or struggling with a painful situation. I stop mid-criticism, smile at myself, and say, "Good morning, beautiful!" I feel grateful to my critical voice for the reminder to find compassion for myself, focus on what's important, and get on with my day.

The moments when you turn the difficult experiences of the world on yourself and see ugliness are your prompts to *reach deeply* for whatever it is that brings you back to knowing your beauty. And remember, searching for your flaws only leads to seeing more ugliness in the world, while meditating on your beauty (even finding just one thing about yourself to appreciate) allows you to see the magnificence that exists both in and around you.

Connect with a Body Positive Community

Being in a supportive community offers one of the easiest ways to quiet your critical voice and see your own beauty. That's why the fifth Competency of the Be Body Positive Model is *Build Community*. What a spectacular experience it is to witness individuals—diverse in myriad ways—radiate their authentic beauty in an environment where comparison, judgment, and other social sanctions have been removed. The depth of connection is profound.

You can create this type of connection in your own life. Spending time with people who are committed to using their creativity and imagination to expand society's limited view of beauty is an excellent way to remember your own. When you are overwhelmed with media imagery, or have been hurt by the comments or actions of others and feel the need to "fix" yourself, these friends can mirror back to you your true reflection. They can shore you up so you don't fragment into "flawed" body parts; they are there to help you see yourself as a beautiful, whole human being.

"Being with a group of Body Positive people, you don't have to worry about anything. The relationships are about who we are as people. Walking into a room so filled with love, and being around

people who see who you truly are on the inside, makes everyone (including myself) feel amazing on the outside as well. You feel good, so you can move and laugh and embrace who you are inside and out. It makes you feel safe to feel attractive."

—Lily S., Body Positive leader

Consciously Look for Beauty

Author and artist J. Ruth Gendler reminds us in her book *Notes on the Need for Beauty* that, "as we see more deeply, we find beauty in unexpected places." I believe it is important to slow down (even if only occasionally) to take in the magnificence that is ever present in our world. Yes, life is busy, and it's easy to say we don't have time to stop and look around. We do have the time— it's how we choose to spend our time that is up to us. When life feels flat, stopping for a few seconds every now and then to take in the color and fragrance of a flower or the smile on a kind person's face brings us into the present moment where abundant beauty exists. The more we do this, the more capable we are of expanding our vision to include ourselves.

It takes conscious practice to change how you see. At first, you must continuously remind yourself to slow down enough to see old things in a new way. With time, however, it will become second nature.

I entered perimenopause at the same time Carmen began puberty. Simultaneously, we were living in changing bodies. Our transformation included the addition of new flesh and therefore the need for new clothing. A shopping trip was in order. As Carmen and I stood next to each other before the dressing room mirror, I recognized how easy it would be to compare my aging body to her youthful one and see ugliness in myself. So I stopped focusing on the clothes for a moment and stared at our reflections, asking myself to take in each one without judgment.

embody

In that moment, I simply decided that *both of us were allowed to be beautiful*. Believing that beauty was only for the young was a product of social conditioning, and it was my choice to say, "No thanks. I don't believe you anymore," to the voice in my head. How liberating it was to see beauty in my experienced flesh as well as in my daughter's developing body. Although I didn't speak out loud about my experience in the moment, Carmen and I did have a conversation back in the car about what it's like to have one's body change so suddenly. We honored that it wasn't easy to be in transition, and that trying to find the right style of clothing to fit our new life stages was a challenge.

A few days later, my mom (who at that time was in her late seventies) came for a visit. At dinner, there was a split second when I looked at her sitting next to Carmen in the candlelight and saw them switch bodies. It was a profound experience to see my mom as she was in her youth and my daughter as an old woman. My body was somewhere in the middle. In the timelessness of the moment, I saw the essence of our genetics in all three generations; I was changed forever. It showed me that the experience of beauty is simply a matter of choosing how we use our vision.

I tell this story to let you know it really is possible to appreciate your physical self in a mirror's reflection. You *can* learn to look at your image in a photo or see yourself on video and choose not to attack yourself. The trick is to consciously breathe in truth while exhaling out the illusion that beauty is not allowed for you. You have a choice in these moments to expand your definition beyond the images fed to you by mass media and advertising. It is up to you to choose love over fear: fear = ugliness, love = beauty. If you see ugliness, that's okay. Keep practicing. Change your vision in the next moment. And the next... If clothes you are trying on don't fit well, do not take it out on your body; it's not your body's fault. Dare to be unique and find clothes that feel right for you, even if they don't match current, trendy styles.

MARANDA BARRY

BODY POSITIVE LEADER

At the age of fourteen, I really thought I was open-minded about beauty, but the appreciation was totally cerebral. I never actually felt the beauty in different sorts of bodies, never experienced it with my senses.

Just before graduating high school, I began interning with The Body Positive. I was going through what seemed like a million changes at that time, and, needing an outlet for my confusion, I got into visual art. I drew pastel landscapes of the Mono Lake Basin desert, created twisting patterns in the Stinson Beach sand, and made a variety of abstract watercolor paintings in my bed at night. The more weeks I spent with the self-loving, diversely-bodied individuals of The Body Positive, the more I grew to see them as works of natural art, and I examined them with the same close attention I gave to patterned sticks and the tender ridges on the inside walls of a bell pepper.

As a kid, I liked to soften my gaze completely until my eyes lost focus and things became abstract, Rothko-esque blobs, no longer defined by their everyday purposes. At seventeen, I discovered that by letting my mind relax in the same way, I could stop measuring beauty by how closely somebody fit the "ideal" and start going by pure visual intrigue. There were so many entrancing things I had completely dismissed!

Aside from their fascinating appearances, I found culturally-shamed body parts especially beautiful because of what they represented. Wrinkles, for instance, are unique records of every expression over one's life delicately crinkling and creasing into deep, firm lines. My mother expresses embarrassment about the loose flesh of her belly, but it is a product of all the stretching that allowed her to give birth to me, the squishy softness a symbol of the strength and flexibility that parenthood requires. My best friend's scars are another wonder, because they show the body's amazing ability to heal, if only partially at times. My great uncle's age spots show a long existence of growing and learning, having access to memories of a time that I know I can never touch. And noticing these parts on others makes me understand the true beauty in what I used to call my flaws. I love my funny ears that stick out, the intensity of my facial expressions, my straight hips and subtle curves, the fast-growing hair under my arms, and my short legs.

Like everyone, I am a natural wonder, deserving of awe. And it's so much more fun to live with this knowledge, because I can actually experience the loveliness of those around me rather than acknowledging it vaguely with my head turned away. I see truly exciting things, and others feel delighted when I tell them what I see. We are breathtakingly beautiful when we let ourselves be.

Explore the Concept of Attraction

"The best and most beautiful things in the world cannot be seen or even touched. They must be felt with the heart."

—Helen Keller

In our society, beauty is often linked and limited to physical appearance. The quality of *attraction*, however, is what draws people to one another. Attraction is defined as "the action or power of evoking interest, pleasure, or liking for someone or something."[10] Nowhere in this definition does it say that in order to be attracted to someone—or to be attractive—a person must have one particular appearance.

Many people who attend Body Positive workshops and lectures come back with stories about how their physical bodies are perceived differently by others after spending time with us, even after a short lecture. Their friends ask them if they've done something to change themselves because they "look great." The transformation that takes place in such a short time is not with their hairstyles, clothes, or weight. What their friends observe, but cannot properly name, is an increase in self-love and willingness to see their own beauty. It is this positive change in self-perception and greater appreciation for themselves "as is" that causes an energetic shift that others are attracted to but cannot identify, because they are so used to focusing on specific physical traits.

Distinguishing between attraction and a social construct of beauty lets you physically express what you are feeling emotionally. You don't always have to be "on." You may have days when you don't feel like being seen. On these days, you can go about your life from a more internal, private place. When you are feeling full of light and energy, you become more visible and can engage more actively with others.

Seeing beauty as alive and vital attracts it to you. Sarah Lewin, whose story you read earlier, once said, "Beauty is something that breathes and lives. Beauty is in living." I love Sarah's concise, elegant statement because it perfectly describes my own experience. Playing in the hills above my home is a favorite activity that provides me with a true mirror. I wrote the following passage on a scrap of paper while sitting in my car after returning from one of my hikes through the forest:

"In this moment I am muddy, sweaty, and stinky from my playtime in the hills, and I feel radiant. I saw my reflection today in the vibrant green hue of the newly sprouted grass, the pumpkin-colored mushrooms growing boldly on a fallen log that blocked the trail, and the heightened colors of the eucalyptus tree bark still damp from a week of rain. If someone were to write about my beauty, I would wish to be described in this moment. I am alive and in love with life!"

Redefine Perfection

Author Haruki Murakami wrote a line about perfection in his novel *Kafka on the Shore* that aptly describes my perception of human beauty. One of his characters says, "...a certain type of perfection can only be realized through a limitless accumulation of the imperfect." He was speaking about Shubert's Sonata in D, which he believed was never played perfectly by the multitude of pianists he heard try. He was encouraged, however, by what he described as "this limit of being human" and saw the accumulation of the performances he attended (each played with faults) as making the piece perfect.

Perfection seen as the "limitless accumulation of the imperfect." Isn't that what human beauty—human life—really is? I perceive our experience on this planet with awe because it is a wonder to me that we even have these amazing bodies and brains, so intricately created with parts interconnected in ways we don't even notice or cannot fathom. We get a cut and our body heals itself. We breathe in and out without sending a signal to our lungs to do so. Our brains grow and we learn at a pace that is nearly impossible to comprehend. We are, each and every one of us, a physical miracle. And we are completely and beautifully flawed.

I am inspired by Murakami's character to rethink what perfection means. Contrary to what you are told, you are ideal *because of your imperfections*. You will most likely not do everything flawlessly each day, and you may not look perfect as the word is defined by society. However, each day you are alive adds to the one before, and these days combine to become your life. Can you see the accumulation of these imperfect days you string together on this planet as beautifully complete?

Play with Beauty Messages

Another way to transform your perception of beauty is to collect imagery that makes you feel good about yourself. Close the magazine and take photos of what is beautiful to your own eyes. Write your own articles about how to achieve more love and beauty in your life, remembering to discard any language that refers to the need to change yourself or lose weight before you can have what you desire. Write love notes to yourself and put them up around your house. Search for inspiring images and quotes from other people to add to your collection.

I once had a mirror in my house that for some reason brought out my critical voice. Every time I walked by, I silently criticized my thighs. One day I became conscious of how cruel the voice inside my head sounded, so I covered the mirror with beautiful photos of flowers, my family and friends, and myself as a young child with my pony. The latter represented the time in my life before I was told something was wrong with having muscular thighs, a time when I was still thrilled to use my body for fun. The photo reminded me that my dislike of my thighs was a learned behavior, not an innate belief. If it was learned, it could be unlearned. After covering the mirror, I made it a practice to say something loving when I passed by.

If you're feeling bold you can put the positive messages you collect on post-it notes and stick them up in public dressing rooms and bathrooms to inspire others to see their beauty. Body image groups all over the country are taking this action.[11] Imagine what it would be like if every time you walked into a dressing room you were given a positive message about your beauty instead of feeling isolated with the mirrors and your critical thoughts!

A fun activity I do to counteract negative media messages about beauty is to cover up insulting magazines when I go to the grocery store. If I don't like the messages I see as I'm standing in line waiting to pay for my food, I place political, travel, or cooking magazines in front. I'm not willing to stand passively in line absorbing the negativity of the magazines if there is something I can do about it. People sometimes give me odd looks as I perform this deed, but I'm not bothered because I have too much fun being a rebel. My magazine sabotage has led me into interesting conversations with fellow shoppers about the purpose behind my action. I don't destroy property; I just rearrange the displays so I feel better about the time I spend in a store that is receiving my money. Many of The Body Positive's student leaders tell me how much fun they have covering up the magazines that insult their beauty. I love seeing their eyes twinkle with mischief as they describe such rebellious deeds.

ELIZABETH

THIS IS BEAUTY

I am eager to share *This Is Beauty* with you—The Body Positive's online art campaign in which we introduce the stories of people with diverse bodies and life experiences who are willing to declare their own authentic beauty to the world. It was created to invite you to befriend your own body and participate in this radical re-imagining of beauty.

The idea for this campaign came out of a session I had with a new client who cried when I told her it was possible to be free of her body hatred and eating disorder. She said she'd never heard this was true, even after twice spending time in residential treatment centers! I was shocked to hear this. How was it possible to face life everyday without knowing there was a path to freedom? I told her I knew a lot of people who had suffered terribly and were now completely free. I shared information about The Body Positive and all the things we teach to help people love and treasure their bodies. I let her know I would find a way to introduce her to individuals who were brave and skilled at connecting to their own beauty and worthiness. I wanted her to see what I had discovered—that it was possible to fully inhabit one's own body, trust one's hungers and desires, and experience beauty as the authentic, openhearted, and vulnerable expression of one's life.

After that session I realized that what was missing in my treatment of people with eating disorders was offering them an alternative vision. What was needed was a community of people who were free from the obsession of blaming their bodies for their troubles. That was when I started thinking about interviewing people whom I knew were alive and well, and caring for themselves with love and respect. I wanted to collect their stories on video, in photos, and in writing to share with my clients, and with every isolated person in the world who needed an invitation to be free.

So here it is—*thisisbeauty.org*—the beginning of what I hope will become an unending explosion of artistic expression from an expanding community of diverse people who lovingly inhabit their bodies. My dream is to fill our gallery with such variety that everyone who sees it will wonder, "Hmmm, what is my beauty?" In this way they can turn their focus from searching for their flaws to inhabiting their beauty. I hope you, too, will be brave and take the time now to create your own *This Is Beauty* statement, whether you share it on our website or not.

ASTRID QUARRY

Body Positive leader, Australia

Hole, thrashing in the background. This is my feel good music. I like other music. But catharsis comes from Courtney Love's anger.

A jar of honey sits in front of me. I dip one finger into it and lick the smooth stickiness into my mouth. I dip all my fingers in one at a time. When I've had ten fingertips, I put the lid on the jar and put it away.

I'm wearing my favourite shoes, the ones I've yet to work my courage up and wear outside. Outrageously pink patent leather pumps with plastic heels with dark wood-grain printed on them. I love them.

This is me. Sweet fantasy bubbling in my head. Spicy anger that just needs to be released sometimes. And a love of eye-catching aesthetic beauty.

I also like to play at being something I'm not. Or something other people don't think I am.

Return to Wholeness

"Wholeness ... is not achieved by cutting off a portion of one's being, but by integration of the contraries."

—Carl Jung

Authentic beauty is the sum of our parts, not each part seen alone. We come into this world whole, of this fact I am sure. Even when born differently-abled or with illnesses, we still enter our lives as complete human beings. I see children all the time who are absolutely in love with everything about themselves, amazed at what their little bodies can do as they learn each new skill.

As we are socialized, though, most of us develop critical voices that cut our bodies into pieces and trash the different parts as if they were something we'd like to throw away. When we pay attention to the way we speak about our bodies (both to ourselves and to others), we are able to uncover the ways in which we have become fragmented. Our work, then, is to piece ourselves back together. Although some parts may be considered "imperfect," if we make the choice to see how these amazing body parts work together to give life, we can once again become whole.

Kate Finney, the person who shared her recipe for true rest at the end of Competency Two, finds wholeness by reminding herself regularly that the human body is a miracle, and gratitude a healing force. In Kate's words:

> "When I feel bombarded with cultural and media messages that tell me to diet and really promote this obsession with thinness and beauty, one thing I try to do is come back to gratitude for my body. I think about what an incredible thing the human body really is, and our anatomy, and what a miracle this is."

Another way to come back to authentic beauty and a sense of being a whole human being is to make a commitment to ending the self-deprecating comments that can so easily flow from our mouths, especially when we spend time with other people who trash their bodies. It's really not that hard to stop—it's just a matter of staying silent, or stopping mid-sentence when we catch our critical voices in action, like the difficult mornings with my mirror that cause nasty comments to come out of my mouth before I'm fully awake.

Seeing ourselves as whole human beings instead of fragmented parts—a thigh here or a belly there—lets us remember why we're here on the planet. What is your purpose? What brings you joy? Take a minute to think about how you feel when you're doing something you love, something that ignites your passion and makes you forget about the size of your body or how you look while you're doing it—if even just for a short time. These are the moments when body, mind, and spirit become connected. This is your authentic beauty.

ELIZABETH

BECOMING FREE OF THE CRITICAL GAZE

I had a client once who was constantly trying to "improve" her image. She developed an eating disorder through her attempt to lose weight, which was why she came to see me. This young woman had a critical voice that was harsh and demanding. It was important for her to understand the source of this mean voice, so during one session I asked her, "When you're looking at yourself and criticizing your appearance, who do you imagine is looking at you?"

As we explored our answers in depth, she discovered that when she looked at herself, she imagined being seen by a man who was a potential partner—a handsome, attractive, charismatic, and extremely critical man. He studied every detail of her face and body for flaws, and constantly found them. He looked at her through a lens that was mean, judgmental, and focused on minute details. I asked her, "Where does this voice come from? Does your father look at you that way?"

"Oh, no," she said, "my father's very kind and he only says nice things about me."

"And your partner?" I asked, "Is he very critical? Does he not like your body? Does he judge it?"

Her reply was, "Oh, no, he hates that I'm so self-critical."

I said, "So this practice of looking at yourself from the outside, from the point of view of a random stranger whom you've created and doesn't like you—why do you do that?" She thought for a long time and couldn't come up with an answer.

So she stopped looking at herself in this way and decided instead to be creative and imaginative in her thoughts about beauty. She chose to take in the kind, generous ways that her partner looked at and spoke to her. She began to hear her father's loving words. She noticed that her friends were not criticizing her either. She also realized it wasn't useful to pay attention to the girls who might criticize her, because they were not her friends.

She began a new practice where she imagined a person with kind eyes looking at her. Even that seemed invasive, so she decided to stop looking at herself from an outside perspective entirely, and, instead, to feel who she was *from the inside*. By orienting her awareness in this new way, she was able to get in touch with a feeling of aliveness and a sense of a great expansion and energy. She began to see who she really was—a generous, kind, and beautiful person.

My client became free when she let go of the imaginary person who looked at her in a mean and judgmental way, and understood she was just the size she was meant to be—she was made "just right." She never again engaged in her disordered-eating behaviors after that single session when she realized the way she viewed her beauty was a waste of her time and energy.

CHOOSE BEAUTY

"For always, always, we are waking up and then waking up some more."

—Sue Monk Kidd, *The Dance of the Dissident Daughter*

I love the mosaic photographs (especially portraits) that are made up of numerous, tiny photographs, each one it's own unique image. When you look from afar, you see the mosaic as a whole. When you get up close, however, you see it is teeming with individual lives. This is how I perceive beauty when I speak to groups of people. My mind creates a painting that represents the group as a whole entity, with everyone in attendance contributing their own unique light, texture, and hue. I am overcome with how much beauty I see in these moments. The longer I am with a group, the more vibrant the painting becomes.

Body Positive discussions reach people's hearts and souls. Even during a short talk, the freedom experienced in that brief moment together causes their bodies to emanate more radiant light, bringing even more magnificence to my canvas. I have seen great masterpieces! These opportunities to view superb art are why I love my work so much. When people experience self-love (even for a brief time) and can see their own beauty (both inner and outer), and when they interact with one another from this place—a place of wholeness—*this* is beauty!

I recently found a brilliant description of the human body in a novel by poet and author Angela Jackson. I knew I would love the book when I read in the second paragraph of the prologue:

> "A body: it is a mosaic made of colors, shapes, designs, textural arrangements, symmetries, studies in contrasts that collide, oils and water that hug like sweat. At last, I am all these forms meshed so fine, so skillfully, that I am

feeling. At last, I am so lovely I can touch myself, marvel, be stunned and curious and calm." [12]

Yes!

I choose to see my life as a beautiful, mysterious journey. My body is perfect in its "limitless accumulation of the imperfect." My definition of beauty is something real; it is in constant motion, the artistic expression of me. In the painting of my own beauty, I add color, light, and texture to my canvas every day I am alive. I choose to see myself as a "growing up" instead of a "grown up" because this allows me never to lose sight of the wonders of this world. I see the radiance of everyone I meet because I need not be in competition when I am able to see my own, ever-changing beauty. I am a perfectly imperfect, beautiful human being.

It is never too late to revel in your own beauty, to know you are perfect just the way you were made. Shed all fears of being labeled conceited or arrogant. Throw away any definitions of beauty that stop you from including yourself. Grieve for the time you spent attempting to turn yourself into someone else because you let others define beauty for you. Make the radical choice to cease the body-bashing rituals you perform alone or with others. Reconnect your fragmented parts into wholeness and let yourself shine. Take a bold step further and declare your authentic beauty to the world.

BODY POSITIVE PRACTICES

Declare Your Own Authentic Beauty

Now is the time for an alternative—positive—way of thinking about and experiencing beauty: one that is non-competitive, all-inclusive, and cel-

embody

ebratory. This practice allows you to experience more beauty in the world around you, and to expand your definition to include yourself.

INSTRUCTIONS

a. ***This Is Beauty:*** *This Is Beauty* is The Body Positive's online art campaign, created to make the statement that we are *all* allowed to see and express our unique selves, and to share our beauty with the world. Start this practice by checking out the videos, photos, poetry, and essays at *thisisbeauty.org*. Then ask yourself:

- How do the messages about beauty on the website differ from what I generally hear?

- How did listening to the people declare their beauty make me feel about my own?

b. **My Beauty Is... :** On a piece of paper or a page in your journal, write a word or statement to complete the sentences below. Write your answers only, not the sentence. Leave space for a few words in front of each of your answers.

- I feel beautiful when I...

- Something about my body I've been teased about is...

- Something I inherited from one of my most beloved ancestors is...

- I feel self conscious about my...

- People who love me admire my...

- Some one who loves me told me I was beautiful when I...

- I really appreciate my [add body part here] when I am...

- I feel radiant when I am...

- I love to...

- One secret talent no one knows about is my...

- I wish more people would appreciate me for my...

- The strangest, quirkiest thing about me is...

- I feel unstoppable when I...

Now write, "My beauty is" in front of each of your words or statements to form a complete statement. Don't worry if they are not grammatically correct sentences—you can fix them! Keep your list someplace where you can access it regularly as a reminder that this is your beauty.

c. **My Family Tree:** If you want to take this practice further, explore the following question:

- What aspects of my beauty did I inherit from my ancestors?

This writing activity can be done over and over as you uncover more of the amazing aspects of your beauty and are curious as to where they came from.

Note: If you don't know any of your ancestors or don't feel connected to the ones you have, use your imagination to create the ones you want, or find your beauty in people you know. For example, someone who was adopted who did this practice said her eye color came from her dad. She shared the same eye color as her adoptive father with whom she was very close, and this was how she connected to her ancestral beauty.

d. **Sharing My Beauty:** Now, if you'd like, you can turn the writing you just did into your own declaration of beauty to share on our *thisisbeauty.org* website (anonymously or with your name attached). Or, turn it into a spoken word piece that you videotape, or a photograph with a short beauty statement on it that you pull from your writing. We would love to see what you create!

INSTRUCTIONS FOR GROUP PRACTICE

These group practices offer an antidote to the self-criticism that often happens when people get together and talk about their bodies. How powerful it is to be in a group where everyone makes positive statements about their beauty for all to hear! Remember that making positive statements about yourself out loud is not a sign of conceit, but of confidence. Confidence here simply means you can be your authentic self, no matter how you're feeling or how you share yourself with others.

a. ***This Is Beauty:*** Start your gathering by watching some of the videos or reading a poem or essay on *thisisbeauty.org*, and having a discussion about the messages you heard.

- How are they different or similar to what we normally hear about beauty?

b. **My Beauty Is…:** The next step is to give everyone a piece of paper and a pen, and take about three minutes to write down five or more qualities that describe your beauty today. Let the words from the people you just heard in the videos and in the reading inspire you to find your own authentic beauty. Don't think too much; just write whatever comes into your head. Here are a few examples that someone can read aloud:

"My beauty today is my smile that lights up my eyes because it holds so much love."

"My beauty today is my round, soft belly that cradles my vital organs."

"My beauty today is expressed in my strong, muscular legs that allow me to climb mountains."

"My beauty today is my courage and compassion."

Remember that your beauty changes every day, so whatever you write down, you don't have to be attached to it forever. You can add more tomorrow!

c. **Beauty Is Everywhere:** Now that everyone has written down their beauty declarations, you'll want to find out more about all of the beauty in the room. You will all stand up and go over to another person, say hello, and ask, "What is your beauty today?" After they answer, give them a quality from your list. Be sure it's a quality of your own beauty and not a generalized thought about what beauty is. Interview as many people as you can for about five minutes (you can designate someone to be the time keeper). Write down qualities of beauty you hear from other people that you want to add to your own list. Ready, go!

When everyone is back in their seats, have one person start by saying, "This Is Beauty," and sharing one statement from their list. Go around the room and have each person add something to a collective list. When everyone has shared, the first person says again, "*This* Is Beauty." Take a look around the room now, and see how much diverse and amazing beauty there is! It's fun to write down the collective *This Is Beauty* "poem" and print it out so everyone can have a copy.

And, as with the individual practice, we invite you to share your beauty on our *thisisbeauty.org* website. You can create a group piece or help each other with making individual videos, photographs, poetry, or essays to share. By sharing our beauty, we are inspiring others in the world to see their own.

Express Your Favorite "Flaw"

At The Body Positive, we believe that every body part is beautiful in its own way, even those that have been labeled "flaws" by the masses or ourselves—without these "flawed" parts, our bodies would not be uniquely ours. Today, find your favorite "flaw" and give it some well-deserved love. Try pointing it out in a celebratory way to someone you trust, proudly exposing it, or accenting it in some way. What does it feel like to flaunt something you're not used to flaunting?

Nature Parallels

When you're low on inspiration or in a bad mood, and you need a little assistance appreciating your natural beauty, try this: go outdoors and find a connection between something in nature and a part of your body. Here are some examples found by different members of The Body Positive community:

- Cellulite as the ripples on a lake (without which the sun wouldn't be able to show its sparkles!)
- Aging, wrinkled hands as magnificent tree bark
- Soft leaves as the smooth skin of somebody's cheek
- Fleshy curves in an undulating mountain range
- Furry moss as pubic hair
- Dark eyes in the rich brown soil or a tree trunk

How do you see your body represented in nature?

Build Community

....

GOALS

- Connect to others through a shared positive approach to beauty, health, and identity.
- Role model love and respect for your own body.

BENEFIT

Build community to support your Body Positive lifestyle.

....

"There's a debate in our culture about what really makes us happy, which is summarized by, on the one hand, the book 'On the Road' and, on the other, the movie 'It's a Wonderful Life.' The former celebrates the life of freedom and adventure. The latter celebrates roots and connections. Research over the past thirty years makes it clear that what the inner mind really wants is connection. 'It's a Wonderful Life' was right. Joining a group that meets just once a month produces the same increase in happiness as doubling your income."

—David Brooks [1]

We now arrive at the final core Competency, **Build Community**. As you'll read in this chapter, creating Body Positive communities has been a primary focus for Elizabeth and me from the start. It wasn't until several years into our work, however, that we realized how essential and powerful these communities are in supporting people to become free from eating and body image problems so they can live with more purpose and joy.

In order to fully embody the first four Competencies—reclaim your health, develop a practice of intuitive self-care, reach more deeply for self-love, and declare your own authentic beauty—it is essential to build a like-minded Body Positive community to support these changes. Without at least one other person in your life who understands your new beliefs and lifestyle, it is easy to fall prey to the messages that promote inadequacy and insecurity. The likelihood of blaming your body for other problems in your life (especially if you've done so in the past) is greater if you are isolated from others who are doing the work to make peace with their bodies. Your Body Positive community exists to love and celebrate you just as you are in the moment, even with your struggles and perceived "flaws."

A central component of Confucian teaching called *jen* perfectly describes what Body Positive communities provide. I discovered this concept in the book *Born to be Good: The Science of a Meaningful Life. Jen*, as described by author Dacher Keltner, PhD, refers to "a complex mixture of kindness, humanity, and respect that transpires between people." He writes:

> "Alienated by the violence, the materialism, and the hierarchical religion of his sixth- and fifth-century BC China, Confucius taught a new way of finding the meaningful life through the cultivation of *jen*. ... A person of *jen* 'brings the good things of others to completion and does not bring the bad things of others to completion.'

Jen is felt in that deeply satisfying moment when you bring out the goodness in others." [2]

Body Positive communities overflow with people of *jen*! Members feel better about their own lives because they choose to bring out the best in one another. They come together to celebrate life—the hardships as well as the triumphs—and to learn from the unique experiences and perspectives each individual brings to the group. Body bashing is *not* the focus of conversation. Instead, discussion revolves around topics like the delicious flavors of a new recipe, the excitement someone is feeling because they got a new job, the humor and acceptance needed to live in an aging body, or a problematic life situation for which someone needs support.

One of my favorite things about my own community is the fun we have cooking together and taking pleasure in the sensual nature of the food we create. I also love that we often exercise together. Hiking, dancing, taking a movement class, or walking to a local café for a cup of tea and conversation—these are some of the activities we do that lift my spirits. Fun, fitness, and sharing time together are our motivation for exercise, not weight loss or burning calories. We support one another in staying connected to our intuitive wisdom, a challenging feat in a world that promotes relying on outside sources for information about how to live one's life. Most important, we help each other lay down the burdens of self-judgment, fear, comparison, and shame that often weigh on us.

In a world where emphasis on image, perfection, materialism, and competition are causing alienation similar to what Confucius was concerned about thousands of years ago, Body Positive communities provide safe havens where people connect heart-to-heart, soul-to-soul. The following comments illustrate these connections:

"It really makes sense to me that we should love ourselves. I don't see this in the world, but I get it in this community. The Body Positive gave me permission to know that self-love is a norm—at least here."

"The Body Positive gave me what felt like nuggets of gold that allowed me to focus on what I was doing instead of only on what I looked like. I was given permission to love myself without feeling conceited. I felt I was entitled to be happy with myself. Why am I still here? I love working with other people who are committed to spreading love inside and around them. The community has no hang-ups, no backstabbing, or hatred. It feels good. It feels right."

"I am overwhelmed with gratitude for the men and women at my workshop. I gained wisdom that I never received in many years of therapy! I was finally allowed to explore myself in a deep way and connect my very different experiences to other people's experiences. What a gift."

BUILDING THE FIRST BODY POSITIVE COMMUNITY

"With community support, the level of honesty expressed—both raw and enlightened—leads to inner wisdom. The wisdom shared in our Body Positive group feels like a gift exchange where each of us gets something different, yet exactly what we need, from one another. I always leave feeling so honored to have been a part of the group, and so very appreciative of all I've received."

—Cinci S., Body Positive group member

The greatest (and most unexpected) blessing The Body Positive brought to my life was the gift of community. When I was first inspired to create the organization, building a new community was not forefront in my mind. I knew I would work with others, but had no idea that the people who would enter my world and surround me daily would cause accelerated growth and healing in my own life. I set out to "help others" by creating video and art projects to plant seeds of inspiration and hope in teens. Forming my partnership with Elizabeth and creating our first youth-led eating disorders prevention program transformed my life.

In the early years, we gathered once a month in Elizabeth's office to support our leaders in their efforts to bring The Body Positive's message to their peers. During the first half of each meeting, the students explored their personal process of learning to love their bodies. The second half was devoted to assisting their efforts to conduct discussion groups and educational programs on their school campuses. These students came from all over the San Francisco Bay Area. It was a diverse group in terms of background and life circumstances, but we quickly discovered that everyone bonded deeply because they were allowed to relate to one another in an environment free from comparison, competition, and judgment. Many of them said it was the only place in their lives where they felt truly free to release their fears and shame without their words coming back to hurt them. The safe space we created allowed them to confidently talk about their nascent self-love and awareness of their own distinctive beauty.

The teens in our first peer leadership group weren't the only ones healing. It was a time of growth for me as well. Though I no longer struggled with my body, I remained self-critical for myriad reasons. When I close my eyes now, I can clearly see myself sitting on the floor in Elizabeth's office listening to the teens' conversations about the exhilarating but difficult work of shedding their body hatred. I remember the exact moment when it struck me that I still had work to do to strengthen my own self-love. Instead of keeping that realization to myself, I shared my epiphany with the group.

The students expressed their gratitude to me for revealing my vulnerability. They had been holding the belief that there was some place of perfection in self-love they *should* reach by the time they were grown up if they could "just get it right" as teenagers. My willingness to share my personal work allowed them to see that the development of self-love was an ongoing process. They told me they were relieved to know there was nothing wrong with them because they hadn't mastered a foolproof set of skills to remove all negative thoughts from their heads; that even though I was somewhat further along on my path because I no longer bashed my body, I was still a human being working on my issues, just like them. It was a night I will never forget. In that first Body Positive community, I was given the encouragement I needed to accelerate my growth to making self-love a daily reality.

LILY STOKELY

BODY POSITIVE LEADER

Flying down the road with smiles on our faces, giggling loudly as we zoom through town, we are biking in our bikinis. Riding over each pothole, I can feel the warm bounce of my curvaceous body flopping in a healthy flutter. My friend flies ahead with a smile on her face; all cares are forgotten as the warm rain hits our bare skin and the crisp air cools our cheeks.

Several years ago, the idea of biking with my body so

exposed would have been my worst nightmare. Rather than riding down the road carefree, I would have heard the judgmental voices of my own inner fears and felt petrified of what observers might think. Seeing my friend smiling, and knowing her reciprocal happiness at seeing my smile and hearing my laugh is the biggest gift of her friendship. I feel safe, supported, appreciated, and alive.

I'm not saying I need all of my friends to bike in a bikini with me, but that same energy is what I look for in my community. For so many years in my youth, I created friendships that had the opposite effect; boobs and body fat were terrifying when I was alone, looking in the mirror, an insecure, moody, puberty-stricken teenager. A "friend" to share the constant pinching, squeezing, and body bashing for countless hours acted as a bandage to temporarily hide the deep wound beneath. My fear of my body formed the foundation of many friendships at that age. Like a house built on a cracked foundation, the emotional rollercoaster and struggle with my body image and food had little positive support, and those twisted relationships encouraged me to continue my body hatred.

Learning to create a healthy community doesn't happen overnight. It takes time and courage to expose the relationships that perpetuate the fears we hold about our bodies. My commitment to define and develop a healthy community started with my own personal work to quiet my critical voice, to learn to look in the mirror and love every curve.

The more I love myself, the more this energy overflows to attract new friends who share my drive to live with self-love. Life always brings waves of happiness and sadness, but with a healthy community we can ride the low waves knowing we are protected and supported. A true community helps you express your self-love, respects your intuitive abilities, and encourages you to feel all of your emotions.

Warm glowing faces, smiles, laughs, giggles, hugs, tears, honesty, comfort, and support. We bring out the best in each other. We listen, we embrace our differences, and we always encourage growth. It took me a long time to learn how to build my community, but now that I've experienced the foundations of strong, supporting friendships, my community is spreading out all over the world.

INTUITIVE LISTENING AND RELATIONSHIPS

Time and again, we've seen people make all sorts of positive changes in their lives as they experience more peace with their bodies. Committing to self-love and intuitive self-care leads to a deeper knowing of what's right for us in all aspects of our lives. By honing our listening skills, we gather information that helps us become more in alignment with our life purpose.

As we step away from the parts of ourselves that no longer serve us—those that are self-destructive or cause us to be unhappy—we come face-to-face with the state of our relationships. Some may be as outmoded as the behaviors we are leaving behind, in which case we must decide whether or not to stay in them. Certain people in our lives may offer the support we need to grow, while others may not. The key is to *listen closely* to what we know feels right in our hearts, and to make decisions about whom we want to spend time with from this place of trust.

Intuitive listening helps you find out who is meant to be in your life and who isn't. It allows you to know when something or someone is right for you (signals of satisfaction, calmness, pleasure, etc., are sent to the brain) or when something or someone is wrong (you experience moments of physical pain, depression, illness, self-destructive behaviors, etc.). When you can act on your innate truth, you live in alignment with your authentic self—with your soul. You learn to move towards the people and life experiences that enhance your wellbeing; you move away from those that make you feel crazy or cause you to suffer.

I highly recommend making a commitment to spend as much time as you can with people of *jen*! True relationships are formed with individuals who have your best interests at heart. Your intuitive wisdom will help you discern who they are, regardless of gender, age, ethnicity, social status, sexual orientation, or other characteristics.

Developing self-love and giving it a voice does not mean you will necessarily lose existing relationships or friendships, though it can happen. If you speak your truth and use "I" statements whenever possible to avoid making others defensive, your relationships with partners, friends, and family members have the opportunity to grow and change for the better. If this growth is not possible, however, and your self-love and intuitive self-care are in jeopardy, you must find the strength (and help if needed) to walk away from the people who cause you harm.

You will come to honor the grief that arises when you step away from those people who are stuck in old ways and not willing to let you—or themselves—evolve. This can also mean leaving behind and grieving your own beliefs and dreams about attaining an "ideal" weight or appearance. As you release outmoded relationships and beliefs, you create room for new people and new attitudes that give your life more joy and meaning.

If it is impossible to walk away from certain people—especially family members—you build defense mechanisms to protect you from any unhelpful or mean comments (even if they are given out of misguided love) that may be directed at you by those who do not understand the changes you are making in your relationships with your body, food, and exercise. When these comments happen, you reach out to your Body Positive community for support to remind you who you are and why you choose to live with trust and self-love.

The intuitive listening skills I developed to positively transform my struggles with food and exercise transmitted directly to all parts of my life, but especially to my relationships with other people. I began to recognize a subtle inner knowledge about what was true for me and fitting for my life path.

When I made the choice to heal, I knew I needed support from others, so I began telling my friends and family about what was going on in my life. This revelation caused many of my relationships to change, and not all of them in positive ways. It was the start of a big shift in my community. My commitment to healing allowed me to develop the voice I needed to speak my truth, and that often meant disappointing people who had certain expectations of me. At times, it was scary to hear the words that came out of my mouth, especially the ones that contradicted the wants and desires of other people. This new voice was tentative and awkward at first. Over time, though, and with positive reinforcement, it grew in strength and clarity.

The most difficult choice I made was to leave my partner of four years. I knew I had to, however, because he was an integral part of my eating and exercise problems. Though many aspects of our relationship were lovely, his own lack of self-esteem prevented him from seeing how his comments about my body were destructive to my physical and mental health.

The sadness I felt over losing my partner and distancing myself from some of my friends was profound, but the reward was that the empty spaces in my life soon filled with new people. I was instinctively drawn to those who encouraged my healing and engaged with me as a whole human being. The love given to me by my new friends was a significant force that helped me step away from my obsession with the size and shape of my body. Their words and smiles reflected back to me my genuine image, and I liked what I saw. In their eyes, I was whole and worthy of love, no changes necessary.

I can't say every choice I made during that time in my life was completely conscious. It was evident, though, that seeds of self-love had been planted, and there was no turning back.

One important relationship I developed at that time was with a man who had been a co-worker and friend for two years. Jim had always been kind to me and made me laugh during the hours we spent together at work; it was evident he truly respected his female friends and partners. I was intrigued!

When I told Jim about my eating problem, he didn't try to fix me, but simply listened with compassion and without judgment. Though he didn't fully understand what I was going through, he stuck by my side. We went on dates during which we ate beautiful meals that lasted for hours. His great appreciation for savoring delicious flavors showed me a different way of eating. Through these new experiences I learned to feel comfortable digesting my meals without a constant fear of gaining weight. Jim opened a door for me, and I stepped over the threshold into a world of sensuality and pleasure with food. It was a landscape filled with vivid colors and varied textures, tastes, temperatures, and smells. My passion for lingering over delectable meals began on those dates and continues to this day.

The love affair I developed with food wasn't the only thing that I carried forward—what I imagined would merely be a short fling with Jim has lasted for more than thirty years. He remains one of the kindest people I know. He still makes me laugh and he continues to genuinely like and respect women. I learned early on in our relationship that Jim is respectful of *all* people.

He sees through eyes that search for the best. His compassion and non-judgmental nature are qualities that have contributed to the longevity of our relationship. He is a person of *jen*!

At the age of twenty-one, however, I was not looking for a long-term relationship. To my great surprise, the intuitive voice I was beginning to sharpen told me loud and clear that Jim would be the father of my children. Being so young, I was overwhelmed with this gut-level awareness that I should choose Jim as my life partner. I was certainly not ready to think about children considering I hadn't even learned how to take care of myself. I was still in the final stages of my eating disorder; my only concern was for my own health. By staying with what felt right and true in the moment instead of looking too far into the future, I was able to tuck the message away for safekeeping and live in my relationship one day at a time. Days led to years and here we are, still together and in love.

As with every relationship there were difficult times, especially in the early years when my young self tried to sabotage our love. I continued to listen to my inner wisdom, which told me I deserved to be treated with the utmost respect, and that was something Jim gave me in abundance. His generous and forgiving heart provided me with a safe place to develop into my adult self. Out of our struggles grew a deep commitment to one another. With the birth of Carmen, our greatest bond was formed. The intuitive voice that told my young self to have a child with Jim was spot on. He was, and continues to be, a superb father and partner.

The key to our continued joy in one another over such a long period of time is our willingness to let each other be our quirky, human selves. Unconditional love means that Jim still does not try to fix me, nor I him—even the things that drive us crazy about one another! We see humor in the human condition and embrace each other's (and our own) eccentricities. We raised

Carmen the same way; with love and clear boundaries that provided her with a safe container, she was able to find her own voice and explore her own path, thoughts, and ideas while still remaining connected to us.

. . .

I tell this story about my own relationships because what I've learned is that intuitive listening allows for more meaningful connections and close bonds, be they with family, partners, children, co-workers, or friends. It provides great opportunities to improve communication with others. The aim is to recognize and honor your own needs and desires, and then use courage to speak the words necessary to help people see your true (and often vulnerable) self. You work to put aside your defenses and listen to others' truths as well. As my dear friend Trish reminded me recently, the goal is to practice speaking truth with compassion. A genuine, more satisfying form of communication is possible from this place.

Thighs
a "wife" and a husband

"My thighs are fat."
> Your thighs wrapped around me when
> we conceived our son.

"My thighs are disgusting."
> Your thighs make the lap where you hold our son
> to feed from your breast, and where I lay my head
> in rest.

"I hate my thighs."
> I love you... entirely.

—Lee Marshall Fagen, NP[3]

QUALITIES OF A BODY POSITIVE COMMUNITY

"It is wonderful to finally be around people who are actively living their lives; to be part of a community of people who do not bond through body bashing, but through focus on living their lives and helping others end their suffering over their bodies."

—Sarah L., Body Positive leader

One of my favorite things about Body Positive friendships is that they are built on the foundation that there is no "right" way to live one's life. This way of relating allows each person to be honored as a distinct individual with a unique path to follow. Without comparison or judgment in the mix, the conversation shifts from discussing what's wrong with our bodies and how we should change them, to what's going on in our lives and how we are doing on all levels—spiritually, emotionally, and physically. We encourage each other to explore the question, "What is my purpose and how can I best express it in my life?" This does not mean difficult situations or struggles with self-love, eating, and exercise are not discussed. The difference is in the underlying premise of the dialogue: *everyone in the group is deserving of love and respect just as they are in the moment.*

Even if people want or need to make changes—in attitudes, behaviors, or relationships with self and others that no longer serve them—they are encouraged to do so by focusing on increasing their self-love over all other factors. For example, losing weight won't necessarily increase a person's self-love, especially due to the risk of weight regain and weight cycling that can intensify the critical voice, but true and abiding self-love will most certainly improve one's self-care. Body Positive friends encourage each other to find forgiveness for perceived "mistakes," and to access the power of their intuitive wisdom to make both simple and complex life decisions.

There seems to be a common belief that it's "normal" for people, especially females, to be self-critical and competitive when they gather together. Many people presume that all teen girls go through a phase of hating their bodies, and that all women are unhappy with their appearance. Body Positive women and girls live to break these stereotypes! They genuinely enjoy each other's company. They rejoice in the good fortune of others because they know their own value and see their own beauty. The men, boys, and transgender individuals who have joined our community also break stereotypes. They are brave enough to express the distress they experience with their bodies, food, and exercise, even though it is taboo for them to do so in most environments.

The love in the room is palpable when Body Positive friends come together. Genuine delight at seeing one another is expressed, and the hugs exchanged are life-sustaining forces of nature! Absent are the scans of other people's bodies to compare thigh width, belly size, pecs, abs, other body parts, or clothes. None of the typical "compliments" are given that highlight image over substance; comments that serve only to separate human beings into competing, isolated entities. Facades break down. People look for and see one another's beauty and wisdom—and their own.

ELIZABETH

COMMUNITY IS MEDICINE

The Body Positive community gives me hope, and introducing my clients to the vibrant, warm community of The Body Positive gives *them* hope. There *is* an alternative to the overpowering societal forces that promote self-loathing.

On my office walls hang photographs of people who are healthy, robust, and widely diverse in their beauty. They give me a vision of what I want for the new individuals who come to my practice. I am reminded to trust that it really is possible for people to be healed from their struggles with their bodies. I can honestly tell my clients that they, too, can have a peaceful relationship with food because I know hundreds—even thousands—of people who have become free.

As long as this world is still so crazy that having self-love and an intuitive relationship to one's own body is a radical idea, we're going to need community. When my clients embody the first four Competencies they begin to look around for the people who can support them in living with the radical belief that they can trust their bodies, see their beauty, and cultivate a deep and lasting self-love. Some are lucky to find *someone* who understands—perhaps one friend, a parent, or their partner. Others learn that they need to create new relationships and let some go if they are to live at peace with their bodies.

We all need a supportive environment (even if it is with just one other person) where our self-love and beauty are reflected back to us; where we have the freedom to be vulnerable and show our true selves. We all need to be with people who don't make us feel confused about our relationships with our bodies and self-care. These types of connections give us the capacity to receive the nourishment and encouragement we need to keep going, to hold on to our self-love and intuitive wisdom, especially when times are rough.

I prescribe community—like medicine—to my clients. I encourage them to attend Body Positive events and workshops so they can hear from people who have worked hard to make peace with their bodies. If they can't get to an event, I suggest they go on our website to watch our videos. I've had clients tell me that listening to the testimonials gave them hope and a feeling of connectedness. It's important for people to realize they are not isolated or crazy by showing them there are others in the world who want to be free.

ALIX JOHNSON

BODY POSITIVE LEADER

A common feeling expressed by people who've worked with The Body Positive is the sense that, all of a sudden, the world seems insane. People comment on others' bodies uninvited, torture themselves to change their looks, and—craziest of all— they actually bond over this behavior. When we're surrounded by this toxicity, it's hard to see how damaging it is or to imagine an alternative. But I've found that building community around a shared commitment to an appreciation for our bodies is one of the most valuable decisions I have made.

Becoming more aware of the intense fat-phobia and body hatred in our world isn't easy. It has made me more discerning in my relationships, more critical of my entertainment, and less tolerant of the many expressions of cruelty and violence I see and hear every day. It's hard, once you develop that consciousness, to go on living in a world that consistently tears you down. That's where my community comes in. We can enjoy ourselves and our bodies without guilt or shame. We can express love and admiration, knowing that what we give doesn't diminish what we get. We can commiserate about the state of the world, and eventually we can change it.

MOVING FORWARD

"For the first time ever, I feel comfortable being me. My Body Positive community is a very safe space, and the only place where I can truly be myself. It is empowering to let go of worrying about what others think of me. It is love, not competition. Being involved with The Body Positive means relating in a meaningful, loving, and generous way."

—Alyssa B., Body Positive leader

As we shift our relationship with our bodies, food, and exercise, the old habit of communicating with others based on a desire to "fix" our bodies is no longer a satisfying or useful activity. We have the opportunity in these situations to affect change in our friends and family members by sharing our new outlook. We can be positive role models to others simply through our commitment to self-love and listening to our bodies' wisdom.

There is an energy—often described as a glow—that people are aware of in individuals committed to self-love. You become someone people want to hang out with and listen to because you emit positive energy and light. Speaking to others about the power that comes from loving your body and listening to your intuition to guide daily food and movement choices reaffirms these beliefs in yourself. Live it, role model it, and get your reminder in the process. We all have difficult days that dim our life force, and we all have work to do on ourselves throughout our lives. However, being committed to self-love and surrounding ourselves with people who want to bring out the best in us makes the joyful days greatly outnumber the ones that bring suffering.

A key ingredient to creating positive community and to making intuitive living work is forgiving yourself when you blunder in your communication with others. As you've read repeatedly throughout this book, forgiveness is essential if you wish to live courageously and express your true self. You are human, and, as such, learn through trial and error. With the ability—and willingness—to forgive yourself, you can be bold; you can step away from your desire to perfect yourself and get on with the beautifully messy business of living life.

I am profoundly grateful for my work each day to help people grow in self-love because it allows me the opportunity to practice what I teach. I know without doubt that my aging process would have been quite different had I not followed my vision to create The Body Positive and met Elizabeth. I'm not saying the only way for you to feel good about yourself is to run an organization that supports people in having a positive relationship with their bodies. All you have to do is find at least *one* person in your life with whom you can be Body Positive on a regular basis.

When we get busy and caught up in the minutiae of our lives, it can be hard to remember to be kind to ourselves. We forget that we are remarkable just the way we are. The best way to remember what truly matters in life is to reach out to your Body Positive friends and make time to celebrate one another. This could mean going for a walk, eating a beautiful meal together, having a dance party, sitting down over a cup of tea or glass of wine, or having a quick chat on the phone or computer. I highly encourage you to spend time regularly with people who are committed to their own self-love and intuitive living. If you don't know anyone like this, commit to making it a priority to find them. You deserve to be seen all the way down to your soul. You are worthy of having friends who encourage the growth of your self-love—people of *jen* who cherish you just as you are right now.

embody

BODY POSITIVE PRACTICES

Building a Body Positive Community

Now that you've learned about the five Competencies of the Be Body Positive Model, it's time to figure out how you can get the ongoing support you need to live in, love, and listen to your unique and beautiful body. This practice takes you through an exploratory process to see what support systems you currently have in place, and what you might need to keep moving towards better relationships with your body, food, and exercise.

INSTRUCTIONS

Take as much time as necessary to explore the following questions. As you gather information through this practice, reach for your courage and take action.

- What do I need and want in a community so I can feel good about my body, see my beauty, and listen to my intuitive wisdom to guide my self-care?

- What can I bring to a Body Positive community?

- Which people in my life right now will support me in living a Body Positive lifestyle? In what ways will these people offer me support? Is there anything else I need from them?

- If I'm not getting the support I need from my current community, how can I get what I need to live a Body Positive lifestyle?

- How do I trust my body to know what it needs in terms of food and movement when I am with friends, family members, or colleagues who are focused on weight loss as the primary path to health improvement or feeling beautiful?

- What can I do to spend time with at least one person who is Body Positive?

- What commitment can I make to myself right now to help me build a supportive, positive community?

INSTRUCTIONS FOR GROUP PRACTICE

Have everyone explore a few questions from the preceding individual practice on their own, and then, when together, discuss them as a group. Continue the conversation by exploring the following questions:

- What does a Body Positive community look like? How would it change relationships between people?

- How will it feel to step away from people who can't support our desire to live at peace with our bodies?

- How can we support one another in expressing the grief we feel when we leave behind negative people, mindsets, and anything else that keeps us from loving our bodies?

- How can we have compassion for the people in our lives who still believe that weight loss is the answer to all their problems?

- What are the obstacles to living a Body Positive lifestyle, and how can we overcome them?

Letter of Encouragement in Your Community of One

Whether or not you have support from a solid community, it's important to remember you can be your own best friend, which is a form of community. This practice gives you the opportunity to provide yourself with encouragement as you embody the Competencies.

INSTRUCTIONS

Write a letter to yourself about your personal journey to living a Body Positive lifestyle. Include the changes you experience in your perception of yourself, and how you may be inhabiting and caring for your body differently as you embody each of the Competencies. If all of these changes have just begun for you, and you feel the need to let some dust settle, that's okay! Be honest, including any confusion or subtleties of your new way of thinking.

Then, seal the letter in a self-addressed stamped envelope and give it to a friend to mail in several months, or leave it somewhere in your house to find in the future. Do this whenever you need your own support. It's a great way to keep a running conversation with yourself throughout your life—plus it's fun to get mail!

Throw a Body Positive Party

One of the best ways to be Body Positive is to gather together with others who are also doing the work to love themselves just as they are in the moment, see and express their unique beauty, and listen to their innate wisdom to make food and exercise choices.

A great way to do this is to have a meal together where you:

- Talk about the fabulous flavors and other wonderful qualities of the food everyone has shared.

- Play games, like eating the entire meal with your fingers, or eating with your non-dominant hand.

- Go around the table and let each person take a moment to share one way in which they are embodying the Competencies, or something they are struggling with and for which they need support.

- If you are meeting outdoors, make it a picnic and, after you're done eating, play tag or Frisbee or some other game you remember from childhood.

- Do whatever you can think of to celebrate yourself and others in your Body Positive community!

What's Next?

"Ours is not the task of fixing the entire world all at once, but of stretching out to mend the part of the world that is within our reach. Any small, calm thing that one soul can do to help another soul, to assist some portion of this poor suffering world, will help immensely."

—Clarissa Pinkola Estes, PhD

Now that we've explored the five core Competencies of the Be Body Positive Model together, what's next? Where do you go from here? Start by remembering that the information offered in *Embody* was given in the spirit of trusting you to take in only what works for you in this moment, and leaving the rest for now—or perhaps forever. I hope you have seen that you possess the innate knowledge to know what works and what doesn't for your unique body and life.

If reading this book has brought struggles to the forefront, you may need to seek out a therapist or some type of health professional to support you in creating more peace and balance. If this is the case, I highly recommend finding someone who practices a weight-neutral, pleasure-focused approach to health who will work with you to enhance your ability to listen to—and follow—your body's intuitive wisdom.

You may want to further your exploration of the topics covered in *Embody* by reading other books or exploring other websites. You will find a comprehensive resource section on our website—*thebodypositive.org*—which will stay current and relevant to your needs.

GETTING INVOLVED WITH THE BODY POSITIVE

There are many ways to further your involvement with The Body Positive. If you've worked with the practices at the end of the Competency chapters and decide you want to explore the concepts in community with others, we offer many different workshops that may interest you. If you are a student or work at a school or in other settings with students in kindergarten through college, you may be interested in learning more about our leadership trainings, introductory workshops, DVDs, and curricula. If in-person participation is not an option, you can get connected through our online programs, *This Is Beauty* project (*thisisbeauty.org*), and our social media sites. Check in from time to time to get a refresher, or immerse yourself more fully in expanding your Body Positive experience. The choice is up to you.

Investigate your current relationships to see if you have anyone who will support you in embodying the Competencies. You may want to read *Embody* in a book group as a way to get others to join you in living with self-love and trust. Try sharing (perhaps slowly!) the concepts with family members, partners, friends, or others in your community. Don't be discouraged if you find that people remain focused on weight and weight loss as a path to health. What you have read in this book is radical work that turns many societal beliefs upside down. Patience is needed to get others to see the value of trusting their own bodies in the pursuit of health and more joyful living. It's not easy to cultivate the ability (and courage) to say "no thanks" to the powerful systems in place that teach people to turn away from their authentic beauty and self-love. But it's certainly possible.

. . .

Remember, you are not only enough but fabulous and worthy of the very best life has to offer—in relationships, in the way you treat yourself, and in all that you choose for your life. My wish is that you take the time you need to breathe, question, practice, and reflect on your journey to knowing true self-love. I also hope you will spend as much of your precious time as you can with others who are committed to loving their bodies and seeing their beauty throughout all stages of life—people who are willing to ride the waves of joy and suffering with you, and who reflect back to you the fabulous person you are in every moment. The Body Positive is creating this world. Please join us.

REFERENCES

All URL addresses were active at the time of this book's publication.

Welcome

1. "double bind." *OED Online.* (n.d.). *Oxford University Press.* http://oxforddictionaries.com/definition/english/double-bind?q=double+bind.

Competency One

1. Dempsey, Earnest (interviewer) & Bacon, Linda (Interviewee). (March 2013). "Op-Ed: No evidence weight loss improves health, says nutrition expert." *Digital Journal.* http://digitaljournal.com/article/345802.

2. *PRWeb.* (Dec. 13, 2012). "U.S. Weight Loss Market Forecast To Hit $66 Billion in 2013." http://www.prweb.com/releases/2012/12/prweb10278281.htm.

3. Guisinger, Shan. (March 2012). "Dangers of Dieting a Body Adapted to Famine." *F.E.A.S.T.* http://feast-ed.org/Resources/Arti clesforFEAST/DangersofDietingaBody AdaptedtoFamine.aspx.

4. Ibid.

5. Oliver, J. Eric. (2006). *Fat Politics: The Real Story Behind America's Obesity Epidemic.* New York: Oxford University Press, 16-22.

6.   Flegal, K.M., Graubard, B.I., Williamson, D.F., & Gail, M.H. (2005). "Excess Deaths Associated with Underweight, Overweight, and Obesity." *JAMA, 293*(15), 1861-1867. http://www.ncbi.nlm.nih. gov/pubmed/15840860.

7.   Lyons, Pat. (Spring 1998). "Losing Weight—An Ill-Fated New Year's Resolution." *Radiance: The Magazine for Large Women.* http://radi- ancemagazine.com/issues/1998/spring_98/making_news.html.

8.   Bacon, Linda. (2008). *Health at Every Size: The Surprising Truth About Your Weight.* Dallas, TX: BenBella Books, xxiii.

9.   The Center for Consumer Freedom. (2005). "An Epidemic of Obesity Myths." http://www.obesitymyths.com/downloads/Obe- sityMyths.pdf.

10.   Dempsey, Earnest (interviewer) & Bacon, Linda (Interviewee). (March 2013). "Op-Ed: No evidence weight loss improves health, says nutrition expert." *Digital Journal.* http://digitaljournal.com/ article/345802.

11.   Puhl, R.M., Andreyeva, T., Brownell, K.D. (June 2008). "Percep- tions of weight discrimination: prevalence and comparison to race and gender discrimination in America." *International Journal of Obe- sity.* http://www.ncbi.nlm.nih.gov/pubmed/18317471.

12.   The Council on Size and Weight Discrimination. (n.d.). "Frequently Asked Questions About Weight Discrimination." http://www.cswd. org/docs/faq.html.

13.   *Library Index.* (n.d.). "Legal Political and Social Issues of Over- weight and Obesity—Weight-based Discrimination." http://www. libraryindex.com/pages/1224/Political-Legal-Social-Issues-Over- weight-Obesity-weight-based-discrimination.html.

14.   Ferguson, Mary. (n.d.). "A Growing Problem: Race, Class and Obesity Among American Women." New York University. http:// journalism.nyu.edu/publishing/archives/race_class/othergirls- stuff.html.

15.   Bacon, Linda. (2008). *Health at Every Size: The Surprising Truth About Your Weight.* Dallas, TX: BenBella Books, 63.

16.   Flum, David R., Salem, Leon, Broeckel Elrod, Jo Ann, Dellinger, E. Patchen, Cheadle, Allen, & Chan, Leighton. (2005). "Early mor-

tality among Medicare beneficiaries undergoing bariatric surgical procedures." *JAMA, 294*(15), 1903–1908. http://jama.jamanetwork.com/article.aspx?articleid=201707.

17. Lyons, Pat. (2009). "Prescription for Harm: Diet Industry Influence, Public Health Policy, and the 'Obesity Epidemic.'" In *The Fat Studies Reader,* edited by Esther Rothblum and Sondra Solovay. New York: New York University Press, 79.

18. Zhao, Yafu, & Encinosa, William. (April 2009). "Hospitalizations for Eating Disorders from 1999 to 2006." *Agency for Health Care Research and Quality: Health Care Cost and Utilization Project.* http://www.hcup-us.ahrq.gov/reports/statbriefs/sb70.jsp.

19. Mirasol Recovery Centers. (n.d.) "Eating Disorder Statistics." http://www.mirasol.net/eating-disorders/information/eating-disorder-statistics.php.

20. Bennett, Jessica. (Mar. 13, 2010). "Anorexia: Families Fight for Insurance Coverage." *Newsweek.* http://www.newsweek.com/anorexia-families-fight-insurance-cover age-90867.

21. Ornstein, Robert & Sobel, David. (1989). *Healthy Pleasures.* Boston: Addison-Wesley Publishing Company, Inc., 82.

22. Bacon, L., VanLoan, M., Stern, J.S., & Keim, N. (June 2005). "Size acceptance and intuitive eating improves health for obese female chronic dieters." *Journal of American Dietetic Association, 105*(6), 929-936.

23. Bacon, Linda & Aphramor, Lucy. (Jan. 24, 2011). "Weight Science: Evaluating the Evidence for a Paradigm Shift." *Nutrition Journal.* http://www.nutritionj.com/content/10/1/9.

24. Ibid.

25. Ibid.

26. Ibid.

27. Gaesser, Glenn. (2002). *Big Fat Lies: The Truth About Your Weight and Your Health.* Carlsbad, CA: Gürze Books, 82.

28. Ibid., 33.

embody

Competency Two

1. Rimer, Sara. (Winter 2011). "Happiness & Health." In *HSPS News*. Edited by Madeline Drexler. Harvard School of Public Health. http://www.hsph.harvard.edu/news/magazine/happiness-stress-heart-disease/.

2. To learn more about Prader Willi Syndrome see http://www.pwsausa.org.

3. The Original Intuitive Eating Pros. (n.d.). "Resources." http://www.intuitiveeating.org/content/resources.

4. Ornstein, Robert & Sobel, David. (1989). *Healthy Pleasures*. Boston: Addison-Wesley Publishing Company, Inc., 86.

5. Ibid., 107.

6. Katz, Mandy. (July 15, 2009). "Tossing Out the Diet and Embracing the Fat." *The New York Times*. http://www.ny times.com/2009/07/16/health/nutrition/16skin.html ?_r=0.

7. Blair, Steven. (n.d.). "Fit and Fat." http://suewidemark.com/fat-fit-new.htm.

Competency Three

1. "amour de soi." *The Blackwell Dictionary of Western Philosophy*. (2004). Edited by Nicholas Bunnin and Jiyuan Yu. Blackwell Reference Online. http://www.blackwellreference.com/subscriber/tocnode.html?id=g9781405106795_chunk_g97814051067952_ss1-103.

2. Brown, Brené. (2010). *The Gifts of Imperfection: Let Go of Who You Think You're Supposed to Be and Embrace Who You Are*. Center City, MN: Hazelden, 26-30.

3. For more information about research on self-compassion see www.selfcompassion.org.

4. Parker-Pope, Tara. (Feb. 28, 2011). "Go Easy on Yourself, a New Wave of Research Urges." *The New York Times*. http://well.blogs.nytimes.com/2011/02/28/go-easy-on-yourself-a-new-wave-of-research-urges/?_r=0.

5. Keltner, Dacher. (2009). *Born to be Good: The Science of a Meaningful Life*. New York: W.W. Norton & Company, 222.

6. Wallis, Claudia. (July 8, 2009). "The Science of Happiness Turns 10. What Has It Taught?" *TIME*. http://www.time.com/time/health/article/0,8599,1908173,00.html.

7. Ornstein, Robert & Sobel, David. (1989). *Healthy Pleasures*. Boston: Addison-Wesley Publishing Company, Inc., 168.

8. Macy, Joanna. (2007). *World as Lover, World as Self: Courage for Global Justice and Ecological Renewal*. Berkeley: Parallax Press, 59.

9. Buhner, Stephen. (2004). *The Secret Teachings of Plants*. Rochester: Bear and Company, 109.

Competency Four

1. Orbach, Susie. (2009). *Bodies*. New York: Picador, 109.

2. Wolf, Naomi. (2002). *The Beauty Myth: How Images of Beauty Are Used Against Women*. New York: HarperCollins Publishers, 1.

3. Andersen, Arnold, Cohn, Leigh & Holbrook, Tom. (2000). *Making Weight: Men's Conflicts with Food, Weight, Shape & Appearance*. Carlsbad, CA: Gürze Books, 55.

4. Columbia University's Mailman School of Public Health. (April 14, 2007). "Gay Men Have Higher Prevalence Of Eating Disorders." *ScienceDaily*. www.sciencedaily.com/releases/2007/04/070413160923.htm.

5. Hudson, J., Hiripi, E., Pope, H., & Kessler, R. (2007). "The prevalence and correlates of eating disorders in the national comorbidity survey replication." *Biological Psychiatry, 61*, 348–358.

6. Darcy, A.M. & Lin, I.H. (2012). "Are we asking the right questions? A review of assessment of males with eating disorders." *Eating Disorders: The Journal of Treatment and Prevention, 20-5*, 416-426.

7. Ditch the Label. (n.d.). "Appearance Bullying Support for Teens." http://www.ditchthelabel.org/appearance-bullying-support-teens/.

8. Weaver, Rheyanne. (Oct. 16, 2012). "How Being Bullied Over Appearance Can Strain Mental Health." http://health.yahoo.net/articles/mental-health/how-being-bullied-over-appearance-can-strain-mental-health.

9. Ditch the Label. (n.d.). "Appearance Bullying Support for Teens." http://www.ditchthelabel.org/appearance-bullying-support-teens/.

10. "attraction." *OED Online*. (n.d.). *Oxford University Press*. http://oxforddictionaries.com/definition/english/attraction.

11. To learn more about public post-it note actions see http://www.operationbeautiful.com.

12. Jackson, Angela. (2009). *Where I Must Go*. Evanston, IL: TriQuarterly Books/Northwestern University Press, 3.

Competency Five

1. Brooks, David. (Jan. 17, 2011). "Social Animal: How the New Sciences of Human Nature Can Help Make Sense of a Life." *The New Yorker*. http://www.newyorker.com/reporting/2011/01/17/110117fa_fact_brooks?currentPage=1.

2. Keltner, Dacher. (2009). *Born to be Good: The Science of a Meaningful Life*. New York: W.W. Norton & Company, 3-4.

3. Fagen, Lee M. (2009). *A "Wife" and a Husband*. Used with permission.

ACKNOWLEDGEMENTS

What an incredible journey I've been on since healing from my eating disorder and realizing my vision to create The Body Positive. It's one I certainly haven't taken alone; countless people have given their support, guidance, inspiration, and love, greatly enriching my life as I've pursued my dream. It is impossible to name all of the people who have contributed to The Body Positive over the past two decades. I honor and thank them all, including those who are not acknowledged here.

First and foremost, I express my love and eternal gratitude to Elizabeth Scott, my partner and true friend without whom The Body Positive would never have become such a powerful force of light in the world. I am hers for eternity!

I am forever indebted to Lindsey Hall and Leigh Cohn, my publishers at Gürze Books. I don't think any other publisher would have believed in the project on such a deep level, or have been as interested in my input on its direction and design. To Lindsey, I give sincere thanks and respect for revealing the essence of *Embody* through her loving and skillful editor's touch. What an incredible process it was to work with her.

I want to acknowledge and thank all of the people who supported the writing of this book. Elizabeth Scott, Carmen Sobczak,

Bill Marzolla, Andrea Earle, Sarah Lewin, Sally Friedman, Judith Hildinger, Pia Ghosh, Anna B Dimitruk, Kelle Jacobs, Lily Stokely, Cybele Gouverneur, Louisa LeMauviel, Elena Frink, and Amanda Kessner gave invaluable feedback that helped shape the original draft. Maranda Barry was instrumental in the development of the Competency practices. Lillie Humphrey offered critical assistance with the references. Jaime Mitchell and Kate Finney contributed to the Reclaim Health Competency chapter through a Body Positive project we worked on in the past. Dacher Keltner hammered home the message that the book would be the game changer. My Solano Avenue support team—Christine Mewha, Jeff Armbruster, and Moni Diani-Castillo—helped me come up with the book's working title on very short notice. Amanda Kessner gracefully stepped in and took over many of my tasks so I could finish the book. And my everlasting gratitude goes to all of the generous, brave people who contributed their personal stories to *Embody*; their wise and honest words about living Body Positive lives gave vitality to the telling of this story.

I want to acknowledge the Tides Center for giving The Body Positive a home for seventeen years before we became our own 501(c)(3) nonprofit organization. I am especially grateful to Sonya Watson for her friendship as well as her tireless work as my project coordinator. My thanks go to those who have joined Elizabeth and me on The Body Positive's board of directors in its new incarnation: Jessica Diaz, Adam Davis, Dan Beam, and Kelle Jacobs. And thank you to all of the people who participated on The Body Positive's advisory board over the years. Your help got us where we are today.

Elizabeth and I owe so much to the hundreds and hundreds of generous people who have kept The Body Positive alive throughout the years with their financial donations and in kind support. This organization is truly grass roots and would not exist without their help. From those who gave their time and expertise, to those who made financial donations small or large, every single donor has had a huge impact on our work. I give special thanks to Lenore and Tom Mead, who gave the financial support necessary for The Body Positive to take flight and keep on flying, to Ellyn Peabody, who offered funding and guidance at a critical time in the organization's development, and to my aunt, Sally Elliott, who was there for me with her openhearted assistance each and every time I asked—and even when I didn't! I will be forever grateful to Barbara and Sherman Robinson for believing in my work from the start, teaching me to how to write grants that had a possibility of getting funded, and providing invaluable guidance as we developed each aspect of our work. To Jeff Shein-bein, I offer my thanks for devoting a year of his life to supporting The Body Positive's forward motion.

For their generous support of our research project with Stanford University, we sincerely thank Timberline Knolls Residential Treatment Center, Castlewood Treatment Center for Eating Disorders, and CRC Health Group.

Elizabeth and I want to thank all of the people who contributed to the vibrant look and feel of The Body Positive. Martha Paulos came up with the fabulous name in 1995 when I first had the dream. Dan Beam, Meredith Beam, and Gail Horvath of BEAM, Inc. generously donated their time and talents to brand The Body Positive. Karen Kwan and Jonna Rossi of Green Tea Group used their magnificent creativity to turn the brand language into our beautiful logo. Photographer Larry Dyer kindly shared his time to shoot the extraordinary photos that so amazingly portray the aliveness and love people feel after working with us. He is a master of light! Shep Edelstein has gone above and beyond the call of duty by stepping in to keep our website up and running. And to Anita Koury of AK Design, I give sincere thanks for the way she has taken my words and turned them into this beautiful book, and for so openheartedly working on every project I have asked her to do in the past.

To all current and past Body Positive leaders, video participants, workshop attendees, interns, and volunteers, I extend my profound gratitude. Every one of these people has in some way informed the work Elizabeth and I do. They've touched our hearts with their willingness to trust our guidance as we all work towards having more self-love and the freedom to dive into our lives with passion and purpose.

I give my love and gratitude to Annie Johnston and Carrie Green-Zinn for being such great colleagues and friends in the early days of The Body Positive. Their belief in the work—and in me—planted The Body Positive solidly in the world, and kept my faith in the dream alive and well. And they always kept me laughing! My sincere thanks to Paul Hammond, Gary Felder, and Kevin Monahan for sharing their creative talents and igniting my passion for video production and editing. To my extended family, Lynn Scott and Uma Teesdale, thank you for sharing your daughter/mama with me and loving her so well. And I cannot imagine doing my work without Jessica Diaz, a daughter of my heart and true friend who has given so much to The Body Positive. She fully embodies the work, and gives back in more ways than I can count.

To my Angora sisters and brothers, Katie McHugh, Robin McHugh, David Faivus, Steven Faivus, and Brian Köhn, I offer my undying love and gratitude for holding me in a cocoon of safety and sacredness that allowed me to see and express my true self during the time in my young life when it was impossible to do so anywhere else; they were, and continue to be, my true reflection. I am forever grateful to Trish and Eric Hildinger for providing me not only with their friendship, but also with their beautiful, peaceful home for two highly productive writing retreats. I sincerely thank Judith Hildinger for truly believing in my work, and for last year's exceptional Angora birthday rainbow that inspired the completion of this book. To my entire Angora family, I thank you for our special bond, your support of my vision on every level, and for being with me each year as I rejuvenate my body and soul.

None of what I do in the world would be possible without the love and support of my amazing family. I work in honor of my oldest sister Stephanie. She taught me to look for the good in everyone, no matter their appearance or life experience. Stephanie was a luminous soul whose flame went out far too soon. My middle sister Marcia taught me to be strong and bold, highly useful skills for running a nonprofit! When I hug Marcia, I feel at home. I thank her for all the adventures we have taken together in this life. To my nephews, Bill and Byron, and to my niece, Andrea, I offer my gratitude for the love, light, and humor they share with me.

My thanks to my dad, Bill Earle, for being so proud of me and loving me always. I miss him every day. It may be impossible to ever fully acknowledge all that my mom, Andrea Earle, has given to me. She is my closest friend, mentor, and therapist, my inspiration and my joy. I say this to her all the time, but will repeat my words here: it would be impossible to do any of what I do in life without her patient love and willingness to listen. She forever guides me back to knowing who I am and my purpose in life.

My path would never have been shown to me had it not been for Carmen, my bright and shining star. My radiant daughter came into the world knowing exactly what she wanted, and, from the start, set her sights on big dreams. She is intuitive as well as logical, both brilliant and creative, and she has the most beautiful heart. I want to grow up to be just like her! Nothing in my life has been better than being her mama. Finally, I owe more than can ever be expressed to my amazing partner in life, Jim Sobczak. If it weren't for his steadfast, loyal love and support,

I would not have been able to devote myself to my life's work. Jim's contribution to The Body Positive is as big as my own. His humor makes me insanely happy, and his love keeps my feet firmly planted on the earth.

ABOUT THE AUTHOR

Connie Sobczak is a mentor, writer, and award-winning video producer. Her experience with an eating disorder in her teen years and the death of her sister Stephanie inspired her life's work to create a world where all people are free to love their bodies.

In 1996, she and Elizabeth Scott, LCSW, co-founded The Body Positive, a nonprofit organization that teaches people to experience radical self-love, inhabit their unique beauty, and reconnect to the voice of wisdom within that offers freedom to live with purpose and passion.

Connie is a leader of the movement to prevent eating problems and improve the self-image of youth and adults through her videos, writing, workshops, and peer-led programs for students in middle school through college. Her video *Discover* Your *Healthy Weight* was a grand festival award winner in the 2009 Berkeley Video & Film Festival. She was a 2008 semi-finalist for a Volvo for Life award honoring "real-life heroes."

A California native, Connie currently resides in the San Francisco Bay Area with her partner, Jim. Their daughter, Carmen, is her inspiration and her joy.

FOR MORE INFORMATION
ABOUT THE BODY POSITIVE, VISIT
THEBODYPOSITIVE.ORG.